D0083378

Real-Life Stories from Around the World
Of Language Learning and Missionary Ministry
By Those who are Learning
Through Community Relationships

Edited by
Tom & Betty Sue Brewster

Dedicated to Steve & Martha Green
Who are Betty Sue's Parents
and who have learned a foreign language
through community relationships

135 N. Oakland #91, Pasadena, CA 91182

Printed in the U.S.A.

The people and events in these narratives are true.
To protect individuals, fictitious names
have occasionally been used.

Photos courtesy of the authors in whose articles they appear.
Photos in Balkam's article courtesy of **World Christian** Magazine.

Library of Congress Cataloging in Publication Data

Main entry under title:

Community is my language classroom!

1. Language and languages--Study and teaching--Social aspects --Addresses, essays, lectures.
2. Mission--Addresses, essays, lectures. I. Brewster, Tom, 1939- . II. Brewster, Betty Sue, 1943- .
P53.8.C66 1985 418'.007 85-23884
ISBN 0-916636-06-2

Contents

Table of Contents *(continued)*

Acknowledgements

Many hundreds from our classes have implemented community language learning in virtually every corner of the world. Many of their stories should be on these pages. A special word of appreciation goes to the ones who have made this book possible by sharing their stories with us. May we also express our appreciation to the mission boards of our contributors. Thank you for fostering an atmosphere that enabled them to learn and minister.

Steve Balkam helped with much of the early editing of *Community is My Language Classroom* and contributed to setting the tone of the book. We appreciate the many hours he spent typing, editing, and writing letters as we were getting this project underway. Thank you, Steve.

We have been somewhat overwhelmed by the enthusiasm demonstrated by so many for this project. We have received many other fine manuscripts but the limitations of space have made it impossible to include more. However, we do want to say a special thank you for the contributions we received from: Clark and Anne Peddicord, Tim and Sue Anne Fairman, Doug and Penny Lucas, Nancy Pryor, Jan and Esther Nieder-Heitmann, Bob and Carolyn Thomas, Braam and Willemien LeRoux, Tom and Mary Holman, Jim and Gretchen Wilce, Dick Loving, Ken and Norita Erickson, Steve Kovic, Phil Lamb, and Koos Louw.

Special thanks to Jessie Munniks for her typing of many of these chapters, and for her capable office management that made it possible for us to devote time to this book.

Jedidiah Brewster loaned his father and mother to this project for many, many weeks. We are thankful for his cheerful and co-operative spirit even during those times when, as any five-year-old, he would have preferred to have us to himself.

The truly indispensable people for community language learners are the many local people who have been friends and helpers to the new learners, welcoming them into their community, making them feel at home, and helping them learn the intricacies of their language and culture.

Your editors are thankful for the milestones, experiences and people along the way that have significantly shaped the direction of our ministry and our attitudes. Among these are Nathan Booth, who in the mid-60's, as director of the Spanish Language School in Guadalajara, Mexico, invited us to be assistant directors of that school. We have also been greatly influenced over the years by both the writings of and personal contact with people like Eugene A. Nida, William A. Smalley, and Donald K. Smith. A milestone was the international experience gained in our association with Steve Douglass and Campus Crusade for Christ.

We are indebted to Donald N. Larson, more than to any other, for the philosophical foundation and perspectives on language learning which we received through our teaching association with him at the Toronto Institute of Linguistics from 1968-78. Two other friends, David McClure of the Summer Institute of Linguistics and Dwight Gradin of Missionary Internship, have both provided a consistent sounding–board and encouragement as our language learning philosophies and approaches developed.

We have also been greatly challenged and affirmed by each of our colleagues at the School of World Mission at Fuller Seminary, where we have been privileged to be part of the faculty since 1976. We especially want to express our appreciation for the encouragement and affirmation of our dean, Paul E. Pierson.

Hugh James and Stephanie Young were valuable consultants in the design of the cover, and David Woodward offered the suggestion that led to the title.

For each of these, we give thanks to the Lord.

Foreword

By Don Richardson

Even the most discouraged language "studier" feels a refreshing breeze blowing across these pages. As missionaries to the Sawi, a remote tribe of Irian Jaya, Carol and I, with only 12 weeks training in a summer SIL course in descriptive linguistics, learned Sawi by the social-interaction method the Brewsters advocate — not because anyone told us to, but simply because no one arranged any other method!

In July, 1962 we beached our dugout and built a little "thatch box" of a home among 800 Sawi. They danced around us, almost non-stop, for three days and three nights! From then on, it was total immersion. We spoke English to each other, to our infant son Stephen, and to other missionaries on a brief daily radio schedule. ***All other speech had to be in Sawi!***

When wars erupted. When friends took sick or died. When Kigo needed help patching a hole in a dugout canoe he'd been carving for weeks. When parents brought their children to see us up close, so they'd know we weren't ghosts. When a young woman was in tears because her father had just promised her in marriage to an aged man. When we evangelized. Counseled. Baptized. Translated Scripture. Trained leaders and workers. Built an airstrip. A school. A clinic. A bridge. A dock. When we had to explain government ruling the Sawi didn't understand. For these and a score of other activities our only means of communication was the Sawi language.

Carol and I look back upon the bridging of the gulf that once separated us from the Sawi (along with the growth of our own relationship and the raising of our four children) as the most meaningful and rewarding quest we've ever shared before God.

We are glad God placed Tom and Betty Sue Brewster in the Body as helpers for those God has appointed to bridge the thousands of linguistic gaps that still separate us all from the fulfillment of the Great Commission.

Don Richardson

Don Richardson

Introduction

"**Hey,** I think I might be able to learn a language this way!" This book is intended to give you, the reader, a sense of optimism about learning a language through cross-cultural relationships. We have pulled together a number of voices from around the world to share the adventure, the effectiveness, and the ministry benefit of a community-based approach to language learning that, in recent years, has been growing in popularity. We want you to be able to say, "Yes, I think I can do it too."

Many English speakers feel that they probably couldn't learn to speak another language. In fact, Ralph Winter of the United States Center of World Mission has said that fear of language learning is the major factor that causes many who are called to the mission field to choose to stay home.

Why are so many of us pessimistic about our language learning potential? In the Language/Culture Learning & Mission courses that we teach for missionaries and others who are interested in missions we often like to ask, "How many of you have studied another language at some time…" (then, after many have raised their hands, the question continues) "…without learning it?" Almost all continue to keep their hands raised, even after hearing the end of the question.

In North America and other English speaking countries it is a very common experience to study a language without learning it.

Something unfortunate often happens inside of us when we study a language without learning it. Our self image is affected and we begin to think of ourself as the kind of person who can't learn another language. This negative attitude about language learning sometimes keeps people from being willing to be responsive to God's call on their lives for service in a cross–cultural ministry.

One purpose of this book is to replace that pessimism with optimism. We observe that while millions of people have studied a language without learning it, it is also true that *billions* have learned a language without studying it! In fact, all of us once did it! All normal children do it. Futhermore, throughout the rest of the world it is very common for people to continue learning languages throughout their life time. In many parts of Africa and Asia it is hard to find monolingual people.

These multitudes of people who learn languages without studying them may be an example to us of the way God intended it to be. They seem to show us that normal language learning is not an academic activity, *rather, it is a* ***social*** *experience.*

This book contains the first–person accounts of the language learning experiences of a number of missionary individuals and couples who have learned to implement a social approach to language learning. Each has learned a language (without going to a language school) through their relationships with the people of their new culture.

This book also has another purpose — to highlight the *ministry payoff* that comes as a fringe benefit for those who learn the new language through these relationships in their new community. You see, they weren't just learning a language. They were also learning a culture, and at the same time they were developing many deep relationships. This cultural knowledge and these new relationships often provide significant keys, or bridges, for the introduction of the Good News of the Lord Jesus Christ. One learner, when contrasting her experience with those trained in a Japanese language school, observed that she and her husband viewed the people as *friends* to share their heart with, while the missionary language school graduates whom she knew were not as much at ease in relationships and typically viewed the people as *targets for evangelism*.. She said it made all the difference in their roles and ways of relating to people.

LANGUAGE/CULTURE LEARNING ORIENTATION

With only a couple of exceptions, each of our contributors was trained by us in our Language/Culture Learning & Mission[1] course. Those who were exceptions either independently followed the suggestions of our books ***LEARN!***, ***LAMP***, and ***BONDING and the Missionary Task***[2] or (in the case of the Lovings) they followed these same principles of learning through relationships but they happened to do it before these materials were written.

---

[1]The Language/Culture Learning and Mission course is regularly offered at the School of World Mission at Fuller Seminary in Pasadena, California or elsewhere, upon request. The course is also available in either audio or video tape format from Lingua House Ministries, Box 91, Pasadena, Ca, 91182.

[2]***LAMP*** *(Language Acquisition Made Practical),* ***LEARN!*** *(Language Exploration and Acquisition Resource Notebook!),* ***BONDING***, and other language learning materials for missionaries are also available from Lingua House Ministries.

Of course, non–school language learning through relationships is nothing new. People have been learning languages through social relationships since Cain and Abel, and they have no doubt learned second languages this way since the Tower of Babel. Many old missionary biographies could be cited that show that until rather recently this was the common way to learn. But in recent years the presupposition has developed among many that schools are the place to learn. At the same time an increase in the failure to learn has been observed.

Language/Culture Learning & Mission is a skill development course. Class lectures demonstrate learning procedures and develop the foundational philosophical perspectives that are essential if learning through relationships is to be successful. Class activities give an opportunity to role–play language learning skills and to practice pronunciation and phonetics skills. But the course is essentially a street–work course. Field work is carried out among the people of a different language community and the refinement of language/culture learning skills is monitored through interviews with a Teaching Assistant.

Learning a language and culture through relationships in a community requires a tremendous commitment to the people of the new language. We sometimes point out that if one's goal is to learn a language, then failure is probably predictable. If you are one of those who have studied a language without learning it then you may be an example to prove the point! However, *if your goal is to live with people, to love and serve them, and to become a belonger in your new community, then learning the language will prove to be a great means to that goal.* And learning the language will probably become quite manageable!

But then one is faced with a different kind of problem — "Wait a minute, Lord! I don't know if I want to get ***that*** close to the people, even if You *have* called me to them."

Each one of our contributors has grappled with these issues and has chosen to become a belonger with the people of his or her new cultural community. In the following accounts they share with you their struggles and their victories as they have learned a new language, become bicultural and effectively initiated their ministry of sharing the Good News of Jesus Christ with the people in their new community.

We are often asked, "How long does it take to learn a language this way, through relationships?" We usually respond with two answers — "It depends," and "It doesn't matter." These are not intended to be flippant answers, and both need amplification.

It depends on lots of things: Is the learner comfortable with both the philosophy and the value of learning and ministering this way, and is he or she *well trained* as a learner? (In general, we do not recommend that Westerners attempt an independent approach to language learning without adequate training and preparation.) Do the priorities and expectations of the mission agency result in affirmation and adequate opportunity for both training and language learning? Are the various social factors encountered in the new community conducive to acceptance and efficient learning? Are the pronunciation and structure of the new language reasonably manageable or quite a challenge? Another major determining factor is, of course, one's rate of learning. All children don't learn languages at the same rate and neither do all adults. Some three–year–olds are quite verbal while others may gain more momentum later; however, ten years later those same children will all be native speakers with quite similar language skills. Adults, too, should expect to learn at different rates, but, if given adequate opportunity, each can expect to become proficient in his or her new language.

We also say, "It doesn't matter how long it might take to learn the language." We have seen that those who are carrying out their learning through relationships in community are often being fulfilled in their various ministry opportunities right from the first weeks. They expect that their learning will be in process for a good long time but they are not waiting until some later time to be involved in significant ministry relationships — those have been going on all along.

Community based language learning might not be for every one, but it has been a most enjoyable and effective approach for many who have followed it. In general, we have found that it is important for learners to be well trained before attempting an independent language learning strategy. Nevertheless, we suspect that, given the right training, attitude and opportunity, all of us probably have the ability to become bilingual and bicultural.

Tom and Betty Sue Brewster

Pasadena, CA, 1985

P.S. Some of our contributors have found it wise to choose to disguise their identity and/or the identity of their country

VERMICELLI

Steve Balkam is a lanky, easy-going fellow who was working as a journalist for a small-town newspaper when God put a call on his life for mission service. From the outset he knew he would be working with a group of politically displaced people and within six or seven months after he completed the Language/Culture Learning & Mission course he was abroad with refugees, living and ministering in their midst.

We have started this book with Steve's contribution because it describes significant aspects of the language/culture learning approach, and shares some of the kinds of experiences that most of our other contributors also went through while they were in the process of learning how *to learn languages through relationships.*

Steve's paper was originally written to fulfill a requirement of our Language/Culture Learning & Mission course. It has been previously published under the title "Candles and Catfish Brains," and is reprinted by permission from WORLD CHRISTIAN *Magazine ©1984, volume 3, number 6 (PO Box 40010, Pasadena, CA 91104).*

The Art of Loving Catfish Brains

by Steve Balkam

I was going to learn Chinese, But how? Pulling off the freeway in a largely Asian community, I wondered where to begin.

Dr. Brewster had said, "Just talk to somebody. Anybody." The first place I saw that looked like it might be occupied by Orientals was a gas station. I approached an older man sitting at the office desk. My first contact. How to break the ice?

"Can I help you?" he asked in a thick accent.

"Ah, I'm visiting Monterey Park, and I understand there are a lot of Chinese in this community. Could you tell me if they all live in one part of town?"

The old man's face screwed up in bewilderment.

"Ah, is there like a business district where a lot of Chinese businesses are together?" I asked.

"Oh, you go shambuh of comus, on Gahvey."

"I'm sorry, I didn't understand."

"Here." He pulled out a piece of paper from the cluttered pile on his desk and wrote down the address of the local Chamber of Commerce.

It was Saturday, and the Chamber of Commerce would be closed. I obviously wasn't getting what I needed. The situation called for a new approach.

"I'm trying to learn some Chinese. Do you speak Chinese?"

"I speak Cantonese."

"Oh good, I wonder how you say 'hello' in Cantonese?"

His businesslike face brightened as he saw what I was doing. "*O-ah*," or something like that came out of his mouth, as he waved with his hand.

"O-ah," I mimicked. I was hoping Cantonese words would sound more like words. At least have some consonants or something. "I wonder how you say good morning?" I asked.

"If you want to be polite, you say *'Jo tsun seen sahn,'* — Good morning, Sir." (My phonetic representation of this is only a poor reproduction of the strange sounds he actually made.) As I struggled to mimic his words, he took back the piece of paper and began writing on it the words in Chinese characters and English. Aha! Perhaps I would get something tangible out of this meeting.

"Is there some way to say good afternoon?" I asked.

"We don't say good afternoon."

"Do you say good night?"

"Mahn ohon," he said, and wrote it down.

After trying that word on my mouth, I asked, "And how do you say goodbye?"

"*Chai hoy*," he said, and he wrote it down. He was really getting involved with me. I believe I made a friend, once I got him to realize that as a learner I greatly needed his help.

That day I stopped at several shops and businesses, and made some friends that I would visit every day, as I learned a little bit at a time, and practiced that bit a lot.

That first day of learning Cantonese, I thought back to the reactions of some of my friends and relatives when I told them I was going to Pasadena, to attend a summer mission training program. They thought I was wasting my potential to "make something of myself" by not getting a job "with a future," or going to a secular graduate school.

After I got to Pasadena, however, I found myself being challenged to fulfill a potential in myself far greater than either my relatives or I had ever dared dream of.

I was challenged to learn a new language in a class where the teacher denied being a teacher, and refused to call me a student. I was challenged to learn a language without teachers and without books, and I was challenged to learn a language that might have few, if any, sounds in common with English. I was to learn this assisted only by an ethnic neighborhood where I had never been before, and where I knew no one. Even as I was learning my first words in the new language, I was to begin to become a "belonger" in the foreign community, so that it would no longer be foreign. While still in America, I was to release my Western outlook on life and want to see and hear with the senses of a new culture. And while still an "infant" in a new culture, knowing only a few phrases, unsure in all my ways and having no status in the society except as a humble learner, I was to share Jesus' good news in word and deed with the people. And all of this was to happen in two weeks.

The course was Language/Culture Learning & Mission; the place was the School of World Mission of Fuller Theological Seminary, and the instructors were Drs. E. Thomas and Elizabeth S. Brewster, widely known for their language learning book known as *LAMP (Language Acquisition Made Practical)*. The goal was to become "bonded" with people of another language group through language learning — the key, the Brewsters said, to successful cross-cultural ministry anywhere in the world.

Brewster left the choice of the language we were to learn up to us, save the admonitions that we pick a language we knew absolutely nothing about, and that the language have a good-sized community to practice in. I thought it was a nice gesture, given the skyscraping goals he set for us, that Brewster prayed with us for victory before sending us out.

After my first adventure in Monterey Park, I decided that in order to *really* practice a lot, I had to learn how to talk to shoppers in a supermarket. That way I could practice my few phrases enough to really get them down.

There, my American nose, used to packaged and antiseptic environments, felt assaulted as I walked in the door. I passed by the meat section, where workers were bashing the brains out of live catfish for choosy customers. I decided to use my ignorance to break the ice and gain some acceptance from the numerous people I stopped in the aisles. I picked something off the shelf which my American mind was totally unfamiliar with.

"Uh, pardon me," I asked a woman, "but could you tell me what this is?" I held up a long stick with a waxy, sausage-like thing skewered on the end. People might prefer you ask the stock clerk in a place like that, but they really don't mind helping a fellow shopper. What they don't expect is to find a language learner. But once you have their attention, it's easy to make the transition.

"It's a candle," the woman replied.

"Oh, I thought it might be a firecracker, or something like that." We laughed — then I asked, "*Le sek kum sek kong kuong tung wah?*" (Do you speak Cantonese?).

"*Gno sek.*" (I do).

"*Gno saen hoh kong, kuong tung wah.*" (I would like to learn Cantonese.) Once I got that line out (after several tries), I found that people generally warmed up to me. Having found my entrance strategy, I probably asked about

15 people in that supermarket what that waxy sausage on the stick was.

I practiced a lot, and at first encountered puzzled faces when I tried out my phrases. But finally, I had a breakthrough when I talked to a couple of guys a little younger than I.

"*Gno saen hoh kong, kuong tung wah,*" I said for the umpteenth time.

"Well, why don't you go to Hong Kong, there's lots of people to learn from there," joked one guy good-naturedly.

He understood me the first time! And we had real conversation! That was my first inkling that the lofty goals of the course might be within my reach.

Some of the goals, though, still seemed far off. For example, we were supposed to find a native-speaking helper, or combination of helpers, that would spend various hours a week with us in drilling new phrases, correcting our pronunciation, and making practice tapes for each "text" or related group of sentences that we learned. One thing I learned quickly about Orientals, is that they seem to be very industrious. If I was able to make an appointment for help from anyone, I was blessed to get barely an hour with them before they had to go rushing off to some work, school, or family commitment.

It also bothered me somewhat to continuously pester the members of a Chinese church I was attending, for help in learning new phrases. Frankly, I was uncomfortable with being just a learner. I wanted to serve, to do something for those who were helping me. Brewster explained that as we entered our new world, we were to also become a servant emulating the attitude of our Lord Jesus, who "did not count equality with God a thing to be grasped, but emptied himself, taking the form of a servant." Not really seeing any opportunities presenting themselves, I prayed that God would provide a way for me to help out in some way. Well, God answered more vigorously than I expected.

My second Sunday at the church, I had arrived far ahead of the time of the service, to see what might develop. I was sort of looking around for some kids who didn't speak English very well, because the previous week one of the church leaders had suggested I might give them a few pointers. Suddenly, this same man, Noah, approached me.

"Well, are you ready to teach class?"

"Ah, sure, uh, no problem." Actually, I had no idea if I was or not. It dawned on me he was talking about an English class, and I had never taught one before.

Noah quickly gathered a group of about eight kids in the rear of the small church.

"Do you want to use the blackboard?" Noah asked.

"No." Of course not. I suddenly realized I was going to teach these kids English the same way I was learning Cantonese. "Let's put some chairs in a circle," I said.

The kids didn't know it, but they got a taste of the LAMP method that day, as I helped them to tell stories about themselves in English. The best part for me was that I did not feel like the "outside expert" coming in to teach. I felt like one of them because I had spent time with them and had struggled to learn some of their language.

After the service, where I gleaned what I could from a Chinese sermon and participated in the Lord's Supper with the people, Calvin, a young church leader came up to me, asked what I was doing with the kids, and I told him.

"Oh really? That's good," he said, showing excitement uncharacteristic of the Chinese.

"Sure, I was glad to do it." I silently thanked God for giving me the chance to serve. "Listen, Calvin," I continued, "you know, there are a lot of exercises I still have to tape for my class. I wonder if you might have some time sometime to help me out?"

"You have your tape recorder? We can do it right now."

Calvin stayed after church for about 45 minutes helping me, then invited me to come by his business during the week, to practice some more.

The next day, I zipped down the Pasadena Freeway to Chinatown, eager to practice on the teeming populace the little story about myself that I had learned. I plunked a couple hours worth of dimes into the parking meter, and hit the streets.

First off, I strode into a not too busy grocery store and went right up to the shop-keeper behind the counter. I asked if he spoke Cantonese, and when he indicated he did, I reeled off my story, just like an insider. He waited passively while I told him that I wanted to learn Cantonese, that I had been learning Cantonese for one week, that in my class we learned Cantonese without books or teachers, and that each day my friends taught me something new in Cantonese. I must have sounded like an insider, because when I finished, he asked me something in Cantonese. I was so proud. We were conversing just like friends. He was probably asking where I learned Cantonese so well.

"*Gno mm sek.*" (Sorry, I didn't understand.)

"Can I help you find something?"

Thud. My excitement toppled.

"Uh, no, I uh, just wanted to practice my Cantonese a little." I darted out of the store with cheeks burning.

I realized that I had to be careful about using people as rapid-fire practice targets. I lost the biggest benefit of language learning with people when I buttonholed this shopkeeper. I left him feeling used, not needed. The Brewsters spoke of a child bonding with its mother right after birth as a model of how we should bond with the people whose language we were learning. I had to establish my dependence, and let the people "rear" me in the ways of their culture.

Later that day, I found two old men, passing the time of day outside a restaurant. One of them had gold caps on his teeth that flashed when he laughed. They were chatting on a bench, not doing much of anything. Perfect. I wasn't going to alienate this pair. I put my watch in my pocket and cautiously approached Gold Caps.

"Oh, pardon me, could you tell me the time?"

The men seemed not to understand (perfect!), so I pointed to my wrist. Gold Caps studied his watch for a moment, as if he were trying to find the English words to tell me. Then he just showed me his watch.

"Oh," I said, then I revealed my surprise. "*Le sek kum sek kong, kuong tung wah?*"

I don't think I ever saw anyone happier to hear those words come out of my mouth. Gold Caps and his friend broke out in laughter.

"*Ah, kuong tung wah*!" Gold Caps said, his teeth flashing, and he told me the time in Cantonese.

"I want to learn Cantonese," I responded in his language.

"Oh, you want to learn," he answered in his language with a smile. Then I knew I had won a couple of friends. I told them my story, while they smiled and encouraged me, obviously surprised I could speak their language so well.

After I finished, we carried on a little bit of a conversation with the few snatches I knew. I did have to say "*Gno mm sek*" (I don't understand) several times. But the two men didn't seem to mind. They seemed to be remembering with empathy the days when they were alone in English-speaking neighborhoods, struggling to communicate in a new language, as I was doing.

You know, our Lord had a similar strategy for reaching people. The Brewsters teach that in the incarnation Jesus has given us a model and strategy for ministry. Although He had all power and authority over heaven and earth, Jesus broke into human history and lived on our turf as one of us. He who had known no sin was tempted in all ways as we are, and yet he did not sin. He understands our hurts and our temptations. He's been there before.

Jesus loved us so much He desired to become one of us and share our hurts and sorrows. In the same way, we should love the people, whether it be in Monterey Park or Timbuctu. I have learned that we should love the people enough to enter into their world, to live on their turf as one of them and to be bonded with them by struggling with their struggles and suffering their hardships.

◊

(213)

This selection and the previous one have been chosen to illustrate the experience of learning HOW *to become a language learner. As you can see, even the process of learning how to become a learner in an ethnic community can be filled with the same kinds of joys and anxieties that are experienced in field situations.*

Jo Anne Williams and her husband Bill provide leadership for the Continental Bible College near Brussels, Belgium. Belgium is bilingual — the two official languages being French and Flemish. Jo Anne could use French satisfactorily, but she knew that wasn't enough.

Here, Jo Anne describes her experience of learning how to become a language learner, and gives another view into the general experience of participants in our Language/Culture Learning & Mission course. Now she writes, "I am learning Flemish and making friends in our community." She will also have the opportunity of picking up some of the other European languages that are represented at their Bible college!

Learning *Arabic?*
In *Los Angeles ?!*

---

by Jo Anne Williams

We sat outdoors in a circle, on a spacious red rug. There were about fifteen of us, fourteen of whom were Arabic women and children and ... me! (The *new* me.)

Some of the women wore *Hajgab,* their native Muslim dress complete with elaborate head covering. Maha, Zainah, Samira, Nagwa and Fatima had been helping me learn a little Arabic the day before and the others had been there to encourage me. Now, once again these warm, delightful people were teaching me Arabic, relating many fascinating stories about their culture. As we laughed and talked in the cool of the evening, I realized that a bond of friendship was developing between us and I was filled with joy. In Cairo? or Amman? No. In *Los Angeles*!

A few days before, I had arrived at Fuller Theological Seminary in Pasadena, California where I enrolled in Doctors Tom and Betty Sue Brewsters' class: Language/Culture Learning & Mission. The Brewsters, who prefer to be called Tom and Betty Sue, are committed to the perspective that *"normal language acquisition is essentially a social experience, rather than an academic activity."* They remind us that "millions of people have studied languages without learning them, yet throughout the world billions of people have learned languages without studying them!" In order to become better equipped for effective ministry in another culture, one of our main goals in this class was *to learn **how** to become successful* *language learners in a social setting.* This is in direct contrast to traditional language study (the teacher–student approach) in an academic setting. The Brewsters refer to themselves as Language Learning Midwives, as Facilitators or Enablers, and as Cheerleaders or Coaches rather than teachers; and they referred to us as Learners rather than students.

BEHOLD THE TURTLE WHO MAKES PROGRESS ONLY BY STICKING HER NECK OUT

My first assignment was to locate several different language groups in the Pasadena area and then decide, with the Lord's help, which language to begin learning. There are many language groups in the Los Angeles and Pasadena area from which to choose, such as: Japanese, Mandarin, Korean, Spanish, German, Hindi and Arabic. After prayer and a deep breath, I began my journey on foot, occasionally riding the bus. My apprehensions about starting conversations with total strangers almost overwhelmed me at times. I had no prior contacts or previous knowledge of the area.

What an adventure! I felt totally dependent on the Lord to guide me. Even so, I found myself approaching people with fear and trembling at first. What if they became offended and rejected me? The more I perservered the easier it became, and a miracle seemed to take place. I was *enjoying* myself immensely, and people were friendly and very willing to help. Towards the end of the day, I felt a clear indication that I should try to learn Arabic (even though I hadn't considered it before my "journey"). And so it was that I learned my first three sentences of Arabic in a gas station from an amazingly kind young crippled man from Jordan. That evening as I returned to my room, it was with a song of praise and victory in my heart.

During those first few days as I searched for helpers and communities of Arabic speakers, I met people from Jordan, Lebanon, Egypt, Sudan and Iraq. All were friendly and helpful. They brought a whole new dimension to my life. I was especially grateful to God for the little group on the red rug. As I sat with my new friends day after day, I remembered a quote that Tom Brewster had shared about an African man who, when asked how he had learned a new language, answered, "I went to where the people were and I sat down."

"ELMER'S GLUE!" *No, it's "TOM'S GLUE"*

(What does **that** *have to do with language?)*

Sometimes I call this amazing little formula "*Brewsters' Super Glue*." [We are actually indebted to David McClure for this acrostic, *Ed.*] Whatever one calls it ... it works!

This is the four step *LEARNING CYCLE* strategy that the Brewsters trained us to use for each of the Learning Cycles of the course (and also for our later in–field learning):

Get what you need (a *little* each day).

Learn what you get.

Use it a ***LOT!*** (With 40 or 50 different people!)

Evaluate what you've learned and

Envision what you will need next.

With the help of this powerful language learning tool, I was able to "glue" words together to make many useful sentences which then "stuck" in my memory and "bonded" me to people.

In their booklet: *Bonding and the Missionary Task,* the Brewsters suggest that it may be much better to plunge right into the culture from the first day on the mission field and experience life from an insider's point of view. What an amazing contrast to the traditional language school method where classical schoolroom methods are generally encouraged, and where missionaries isolate themselves for maybe a year of language study. When I had studied French, I personally enjoyed the classroom, but I discovered that — for me — real language learning took place outside of the classroom, only when I tried to communicate with French-speaking people. How much easier that process would have been, had I already had the learning skills I now have. The Brewsters have a deep conviction which has proven to be true: "Language Learning *IS* Communication —*IS* Ministry!"

We can experience joy in language learning if our motivation is to build relationships. As we seek to know and love people of different cultures, while learning their language, the ultimate goal of bringing them to a knowledge of the Lord is reached. This is best accomplished as one begins to become an "insider" rather than remaining an outsider in their eyes.

I CALLED (AND CRIED) UNTO THE LORD ... JEREMIAH 33:3

During our furlough year, I had been calling unto the Lord in earnest (sometimes desperately) for a renewed vision and clearer perception of what God would have me do when we returned to our field of service. I had become discouraged for several reasons and deeply burdened concerning my role in missions. I needed some answers to many long unanswered questions. For example, I had seen many missionaries with a burden for the lost, struggle for years to learn a new language only to give up in despair and perhaps even leave the mission field or minister in English. What was God's answer to this problem, I wondered? Then I faced the question of whether or not I should try to learn another of the languages spoken on our field. Wasn't there enough work to do in French and English? This was only a rationalization on my part. The real question was: would I be *willing* to learn the language or had I already decided it would be too difficult?

... AND HE ANSWERED ME!

A missionary and his family had moved in next door to our furlough home. As he sat in our home one afternoon, he began sharing enthusiastically about an intensive course on Language and Culture Learning that he had taken last year at Fuller Seminary. The more he talked, the more excited I became until finally, I blurted out: "*This is it!* This is what I've been praying for — without knowing if it even existed." We were scheduled to leave in a month, could there possibly be a course in the next two weeks — since that would be the only time I could get free of my commitments here? We called Dr. Tom Brewster right away. "The course starts *Tomorrow!*" This was God's Time. The Lord answered my prayer in this very unique and special way.

AMALIA — ANOTHER ANSWER TO PRAYER!

I had a special need to find housing for the second week of the course, and this became an urgent matter of prayer for me. Since the course is very intensive, and because I didn't have transportation, I asked the Lord to help me find housing with an Arabic-speaking woman or family, within walking distance of Fuller. The day before I was to move, I was introduced to Amalia, an Egyptian woman studying at Fuller. I mentioned to her that I was trying to learn Arabic.

"Maybe we could get together next week, where are you living?" she asked.

"I don't know yet where I will be staying next week," I replied.

"Why don't you stay with me?" she asked.

This may sound simple — but it was a miracle to me. I wondered if the Lord had sent an Angel to rescue me. She insisted I use her car to visit my "little community" and other helpers. She taught me how to make some delicious Egyptian and Arabic dishes. She shared many special insights into Arabic culture and her Muslim background, and helped me with Arabic. What a precious time we had together.

One evening she made a special Egyptian dinner for me. Just before we finished eating, she explained that this meal had special significance — it is called the Covenant of Salt as in the Old Testament. She made an "unbreakable promise" to be my loyal friend for life. Amalia told me how she was certain the Lord had sent me to her. One of the Arabic names she gave me touched me very deeply. It is *Salwa* which means "Comfort." The Brewsters were right: "Language Learning *is* Communication ... *is* Ministry!"

Now I am ready for a new beginning. I know that I will never again be the same person I was before this experience. God has used it to open my eyes to some blind spots and to give me a deeper understanding of how He would have us minister on the mission field. I have confidence that the Lord will use my new language learning skills and insights for His glory.

◊

Here is a fun and easy-to-read article about Wes and Nancy Collins' early language learning experiences. They first spent six months learning Spanish and refining their language learning skills. Then they moved out to a small Guatemalan town and began learning the Mam language. Along the way, they had a number of interesting experiences which they relate with color and humor.

Wes and Nancy were able to have daily language learning goals and yet be at ease in their relationships, not feeling an urgency to "get on with the job." In so doing, they developed a number of friendships which continue even since they left the Guatemala City area to learn Mam. Over 5 years later Wes writes, "We've continued to have neat times with some of our old friends on our Spanish route." When relationships like these are cultivated, you know that you are not "using" people when you spend time practicing their language with them.

We had spent an evening with Wes and Nancy a few months before they participated in a Language/Culture Learning & Mission course we held in Guatemala City six or seven years ago. They had already grappled with the issues of learning and living through relationships and they hit the ground running when they arrived in Guatemala.

Learning Without Schools
Teaching Without Chalk

By Wes & Nancy Collins

• Wes • **As my** friend Jim and I sped south toward the Mexican border, I was quiet and nostalgic. The Alamo in San Antonio was the last thing I had seen that had any aura of "American" about it. Everything seemed Mexican — even the gas stations.

I thought about Nancy. Here I was leaving my wife behind in Dallas — seven months pregnant. And as the August sun grew hotter and hotter, I really wondered what I was getting into.

It's very merciful of God to fill Southern Texas with what He has put there. Somehow, it's easier for me to leave behind the Mesquite trees and tumbleweed than to forsake the maples and oaks of Northeastern Ohio.

Ohio — the colors and smells and feelings and joys all came back. What a great place to be.

But Ohio was where I wasn't. I was pulling into Brownsville, Texas and looking for a phone booth. I had saved up about $20.00 in change and was calling my folks and supporters to say goodbye — as if I were on a one-way mission to the moon.

◊ ***Nancy*** ◊ As my husband headed for Guatemala, I waited behind in Dallas. I would be joining him in about a week.

Life seemed to be filled with first-time experiences. I was seven months pregnant with our first child. It was the first time Wes and I would be separated for more than a workday since we were married four years earlier. We would be living long-term in a foreign country and we'd be learning a language other than English for the first time. For once we would be in the minority and would be ultimately responsible for our own ability to adjust to and learn a different culture and language.

• **Wes** • Mexico was fun — and big — and not nearly as weird as I had expected.

It was around sunset when Jim and I reached the Guatemalan border. I submitted all the stuff I couldn't live without to the scrutiny of a tired customs agent and then stood before a monolithic manual typewriter as we were processed.

We repacked the stuff and tried to start the car.

Nothing.

Welcome to Guatemala.

When we finally got it going, it was very dark. A young German couple begged us to give them a ride to Huehuetenango. What could I say? After all, I'd come to serve.

Two minutes later, I had a growing suspicion that it wasn't nicotine on the Germans' breath. I wondered what it would be like spending my missionary life locked away in a Guatemalan jail as an accomplice to an international drug smuggling ring.

Thus preoccupied, I ran over a dog and listened to the German girl pronounce over and over again in the *only* English she spoke all night, "How terrible. How terrible."

My sentiments exactly.

Next morning, Jim and I awoke to Guatemala's rainy season — fog and drizzle. We were both feeling lousy and headed toward the capital with a minimum of conversation.

When we eventually arrived in Guatemala City, we got lost. I thought that the small road-side signs advertising tire retreading were really street signs. And I couldn't find them anywhere on the map.

What a place.

◊ ***Nancy*** ◊ I flew from Dallas to Guatemala City and after a few days in Guatemala, Wes and I began renting a room in a Spanish boardinghouse, our first step in learning Spanish. Using the *LAMP* book as a resource, we carefully planned our language learning procedure. We wrote out and practiced our first texts of introduction and headed our separate ways on a busy main street to establish our routes.

The stores were small, open-fronted, and side by side, so it wasn't long before I'd gotten to practice my short dialogue with around 20 people. I was rather amazed at the friendliness and openness of the Guatemalan people. This encouraged me to continue.

That first day I found the expressions, "This is all I can say," and "I don't understand," to be quite effective.

• **Wes** • Hugo had a little key shop. He and two other employees were always there chatting with a few friends every morning whenever I happened in. I'm not sure business was real good. No one ever bought keys while I was there. But there was always a lot of talking going on. From my point of view, it's hard to support a wife and three daughters and two other employees doing nothing but making keys at fifty cents a shot. Especially with the volume of business that Hugo had (or didn't have).

I decided to help.

I ventured that a little Madison Avenue would go a long way to enhance sales. We picked up some plywood, Hugo bought some paint, and I spent five days painting a sandwich sign that extolled the virtues of Hugo's keys.

It was a nice way to repay him for all the time he spent correcting my subjunctive and it was a source of pride for me to walk down the street and see "my signs" propped up on the curb in front of the key shop's open door.

◊ ***Nancy*** ◊ Within a week, I had become close friends with a young woman named Emilsa who was willing to be my language helper and help me develop daily texts to tape and practice. My Monday–through–Friday visits with Emilsa became my favorite times each week. We'd chat for an hour or two, visiting with the customers as they came to the small grocery store that she and her mother ran. It didn't take me long to learn how Guatemalans greeted one another, what their favorite topics of discussion were, and what departing words and gestures were proper.

• **Wes** • It was a big help to us to be totally immersed in Spanish — we not only heard Spanish at the dinner table, we heard it on the radio and TV, at church, in restaurants, at the beach. We read it on all the street signs, on the subtitles of American movies, in the newspapers, in our Bibles — everywhere. Exposure. That certainly helped a lot.

One day two fellow-boarders, Alfredo and Francisco cornered me after lunch.

"Come with us," they demanded.

We went down to Francisco's room where they began to lecture me on the fact that, even though I was a missionary, there were lots of words that I needed to have in my comprehension vocabulary which hopefully would never make their way into my speaking vocabulary.

The talk went on for about twenty minutes with all kinds of examples and suggested contexts for appropriate usage.

I decided not to take notes, but the lesson has occasionally come in handy in trying to figure out where I stand in the eyes of a native Spanish speaker.

◊ ***Nancy*** ◊ As I practiced my texts with the other people on my route, more friendships began to blossom — the ladies in the bakery shop, those selling cloth and sewing supplies, the leatherworker and tailor, the store owners and shoe-makers. Each one accepted me as a friend and waited for my daily visits.

Each one taught me a little bit more about this different culture I was living in, and through their friendship and encouragement, helped me adjust to my new living situation.

• **Wes** • Poring over a map of Guatemala City, I found a little spot innocuously labeled *Diamante de Sofbol,* a softball diamond.

I figured that would be a good way to make some friends and get some Spanish practice, so I took my glove, got on the bus and went over to see a game.

I wore my *"Nike"* shirt and tried to look athletic as I stumbled over my lines requesting a try-out. It came immediately. The coach moved me out to second base and hit me a hundred grounders between first and second. In batting practice, I managed a few line drives, so I got on the roster. In fact, the following week I had a new glove, a nice uniform and a starting position at second. That was fun.

My first language lesson came shortly after a pop-up out over second base. The shortstop took me aside when the inning was over and said, "You don't say, *'Yo, yo, yo, yo'* (I, I, I, I) when you call for a fly ball. It communicates, but it just doesn't sound right. Instead say, *'Mìo, mìo, mìo!'* (Mine, mine, mine!) .

That was one of the few grammar lessons I received while on the team. Most of my Spanish education from them was a refinement of that after-lunch discussion I had had with Alfredo and Francisco several weeks before.

◊ ***Nancy*** ◊ My friends helped me prepare for our daughter's birth. Mirna, a woman on my route, was due to have her first baby about the same time I was. She taught me phrases and key words to help me be more comfortable in this new situation. She taught me what they'd ask me in the hospital. She told me what I should eat and why I should stay away from pineapples. She explained that pregnancy was "hot" so a woman shouldn't eat things extremely "cold" (like pineapples or avocados) which could create problems for the unborn baby. It's much better to eat mangos, which are "hot" and therefore more amenable to the heat of pregnancy.

I should also drink milk every day — but just a little. And I should eat fish three times a week.

• **Wes** • Lisandro is a leather worker. He's really good. He can make anything. I took him a photograph of a $300.00 travel bag from a fancy mail order catalogue. He matched it — down to the contrasting trim — at a fraction of the cost. He did all kinds of work for us. It helped to give me something to talk to him about during my daily visits.

Lisandro has five brothers and one spoiled sister. Every January on the first Friday of the full moon, the brothers take a 6–hour trek up Guatemala's famous Water Volcano. They leave at 6 p.m., spend the night in sub-freezing temperatures, watch the sunrise, and return.

Lisandro invited me to go along, and since my Spanish learning goals revolved around getting to know Guatemala and Guatemalans, it was a sure bet.

My only regrets were: 1) That I carried two gallons of water up the mountain, and 2) That I didn't carry any firewood. We had to scrounge for a fire. The only thing we had a lot of was water — two gallons, but we were freezing, not thirsty. Plus, some enterprising Indians (may God bless them) had set up little Pepsi and hot chocolate stands (but, alas, no firewood) every half-mile or so on the trail. So thirst wasn't a problem.

I had practiced a bunch of Spanish jokes that I wanted to tell my friends, so it ended up being a great experience even though the walk was mildly excruciating in the rarified air. I'm still debating whether the sunrise and the view of the Capital are worth the hike.

If I go again, I'll take some firewood, I'll carry just a canteen — and I'll learn some more good jokes.

◊ ***Nancy*** ◊ After Elisa's birth, Mirna and I shared many happy times comparing our babies' development and I learned from her, as well as others, which child-rearing practices are important in Guatemalan society. It didn't take long to realize that Elisa should be kept well bundled, no matter how hot the weather, in order to keep the "air" out. That way, she'd stay healthy. She should never be carried upright or her cheeks would fall and she'd be doomed to walk through her adult life with the droopy cheeks of a bulldog.

I found that this special advice and these special friendships helped me feel like I had a place in the culture and gave me a sense of identity and belonging even though I was far from family and friends with whom I could intuitively relate.

When difficult situations arose, I found that thinking about the friends I had made lessened my feelings of restlessness and loneliness and turned negative feelings into positive ones. Each friend I made helped increase my sense of well-being and my motivation to make a good adjustment to the culture I was confident God had called me to.

I found that, though it was not easy to be away from family during the birth of our first child, these new friends shared my excitement and eagerly awaited meeting the new baby, just as my family and close friends in the States would have done. They helped fill any sense of emptiness that occurred by my being away from "home" during this special time.

• **Wes** • After being a part of the lives of the people on my route for about three months, I decided to memorize some parables and see how they'd go over with my friends. I learned the one about the rich man who tore down his barns to build larger ones in order to hold his harvest even though his very life was being demanded of him that night.

"Listen to this. I've been learning a story from the Bible and I want you to tell me what you think of it."

People gathered around. Discussion was animated.

I had wondered how it would come across to people who weren't all that schooled in the Bible. Their response gave me a great deal of respect for the teaching methods of Jesus. People were excited about the message of God's Word.

Soon afterward, I invited some of the people on my route to attend church with us. Two of them decided to trust Christ.

◊ ***Nancy*** ◊ As I gained confidence and security through the relationships I had established and through my increasing language skills, I was able to fill my texts with the Gospel message to share with my friends on the route. Through my consistent visits, the groundwork was laid for me to share why I wanted to come to Guatemala and learn my friends' language. I had a basis for inviting them to attend church with us. We had established a solid give–and–take relationship where we each felt free to share what was important.

These same friends, made through my language learning experiences, helped me bridge the gap between success and failure in adjusting to both Guatemalan culture and the Spanish language. By being willing to take me into their lives, they had given me the ability to feel and be a part of their country as well as my own.

That certainly was enough to sell the method to us. Relationships are what language is all about, anyhow.

• **Wes** • The Brewsters were never really big on going to school to learn a foreign language, but I came up with a way to a) go to school and b) still maintain the Brewsters' blessing.

I enrolled at a local University — but not in a Spanish class. Guatemalan Universities don't teach spoken Spanish. I signed up for a course called "A Sociological Study of Guatemala."

I took notes in Spanish, took the tests in Spanish and picked up a lot of sociology besides. In class, I would draw a line across my paper about 3" from the bottom. Above the line, I took notes on class content. Below the line, I studied the prof's delivery, noted new vocabulary and anything else I could glean from the peculiar culture of Guatemalan scholarship.

Freshman sociology class is where I learned to say the Spanish equivalent of, "It would be didactically convenient...," a clause which has served me well over the past few years!

The neat thing about studying Spanish through a content subject is that language plays a more realistic part — it's a means, not an end.

A bonus to learning Spanish while studying at the U has been that the prof and his family are now some of our closest Guatemalan friends. We often travel together, spend evenings together and eat lots of pizzas together.

As we went along, I discovered that the *LAMP* approach isn't so much a method as it is an attitude. Every time I would try something new, I'd ask myself if the Brewsters would approve. I'd wonder if they would laugh at me for using a Spanish grammar book for helping to pick up tenses and the subjunctive. After all, what kind of ministry relationship can you have with a textbook?

What I found, was that the Brewsters were not as concerned about the particulars as they were about my basic motivations. Did I really want to *be* good news or just tell it? The ideal was a way of life, not a mechanism for learning a language.

That was a very freeing discovery. I could be pragmatic. What worked for me was OK. So, being one of those compulsively goal–oriented missionaries, I packed my day full of attainable goals like these:

1. Go on the route from 8:00-12:00
2. Spend 45 minutes reading the grammar book
3. 1 hour learning tomorrow's text
4. 30 minutes learning vocabulary
5. 30 minutes reading newspaper & marking new words
6. Listen to tape of Spanish songs & try to follow the gist
7. 15 minutes oral Spanish Bible reading
8. Tape drills
9. Write a letter to a Spanish friend
10. Memorize names of Guatemalan towns, rivers, mountains, and lakes

Of course, relationships and friendships from my route were the core of my curriculum, but by also using grammar books, drills, the newspaper and a radio, I was able to have a little more to say.

◊ ***Nancy*** ◊ When we went to Guatemala, we firmly had in mind that we were headed out to a village area to learn an unwritten language and translate the Scriptures. We knew that there would be no schools in town for learning this new language. No books, no tapes, no helps. Since we knew that we would have to learn this language completely on our own, we decided to first try out the learning approach on a language like Spanish — where we could get lots of help if we needed it.

After 6 months of Spanish I said a sad *hasta luego* to my friends. Wes, 4-month-old Elisa, and I moved on to another language learning situation within Guatemala. This time we were going to learn Mam, a Mayan Indian language.

We found a home to rent in the Indian village and we again began language learning. As I walked around the village, I'd stop in the little stores to learn people's names and say my introductory text in Mam. Again friendships began to blossom as I not only learned their language, but took time to express interest in them and their families, as I bought vegetables, eggs, bread, soap, or medicine from them, or brought gifts to participate in their exchange system.

• **Wes** • People were afraid of us when we went to live in the Mam village. They didn't trust us. Why did we want to live there? At the market, parents told their children to behave or they'd be sent to the *gringos'* house where we would eat them.

Once, Nan and I were out walking. We came to a small adobe house, where in proper Mayan fashion, I whistled to announce that guests had come to visit. A woman came to the door suspiciously.

"Hello," I said. "My name is Wes. Do you speak Mam?"

"No, I don't speak Mam," she answered in fluent Mam.

"What's your name?"

"I don't have a name," she responded.

"Do you live here?"

"No, I live far away. So far, in fact, that you could never make it to my house."

Suspicion.

It was extremely unusual for outsiders to consider the Indian people important enough to want to learn their language. Some thought we were guerrillas. Some thought we worked for the CIA or the Guatemalan army.

But we saw suspicion begin to fade as people realized that we wanted to live long-term in their town and that we were working hard to learn to speak their language. We even wrote their words down in little notebooks and showed them how to spell terms they'd used all their lives.

"The *gringos* are writing our language," they would say with surprise.

◊ ***Nancy*** ◊ I learned how to become an integral, accepted part of another culture through the friendships I made during my language learning experience. I wonder if there's anything as fundamentally important to people as their own language, especially in situations like that among the Mams where they feel that outsiders look down on them and their language. In fact, many outsiders think that Mam isn't a language at all — just a string of noises. I think their acceptance of Wes and me was prompted by the importance we attached to learning their language.

As my language ability increased, I began to share more and more in the Indians' lives and I understood what areas of life were hardest for them, how they coped with difficulties and what things in life gave them joy. I began to get a more realistic outlook of their world view, and, as my understanding of the Mam people grew, so did my feeling of belonging. The feelings of isolation diminished, and I began to participate more and more in village life.

Routine morning grocery shopping walks became an anticipated time to catch up on village and family news among friends. Each advance in language learning opened the way for me to become more accepted as an insider by the Mams. My feelings of being alone and different decreased. I found that we shared much in common, as far as what is really important to us — our children's health, providing adequately for our families, time to visit with special friends. Each new discovery lessened the barrier of cultural distance between us and added to the sense of belonging I experienced as we were becoming a part of community life.

Through the friendships and trust that developed during language learning, the door was opened for me to respond to some of their medical needs. Since I speak their language, people feel freer to confide their medical problems to me or to send a mutual friend to request my help for them or their family.

We participate in the joy of mutual friendship. They taught us their language and ways, and we were able to adjust to their lifestyle and share with them the special skills and resources we had to meet some of their health, educational and spiritual needs. Could any other arrangement be more satisfying?

• **Wes** • After Nan and I were living in the Indian village, we would continue to visit the friends from our Spanish route whenever we were in the capital. We'd go to plays together, or go out to eat fondue, or go to the beach. These people weren't objects whose value revolved around what kind of language help we could get out of them. They were some of our dearest friends.

Once, Lisandro drove out to Comitancillo with me just to see what it was like. We spent an overnight, ate in a small Indian diner and had a great time. He took two days away from work just to go see where we were living and what Nancy and I were doing. Those kinds of commitments to friendship are very humbling and extremely satisfying.

We've come to appreciate that "total immersion" is the most satisfying and effective way to learn any language, because immersion presupposes a social context of relationships — and each of us learned our first language on the strength of those relationships. We were (and are) committed to learning this way — through relationships — not only for Spanish, but for Mam and any other language we'll have the opportunity to pick up.

◊

Don Curry has written his contribution as a personal letter to his friend Sam. He gives us a glimpse of the process of learning two of his languages, Sindhi and Dhatki (we hear he has also "picked up" Urdu, the national language of Pakistan, along the way). Don's non-school learning approach has had a payoff — he is said to be one of the best (some say "The best") users of the language on the field.

Women in the Islamic world face special challenges. In Don's section on "The Fairer Sex and Language Learning," he shares with us some helpful insights.

Don is a medical doctor. After living with the people for two years he was convinced that he could contribute more to their health by continuing in the lower profile of a community health worker while living right with them, than by assuming a more prestigious role such as medical director of a hospital. Two years later, when the story was related to us, his mission leadership affirmed the path that Don had had the courage to take.

The "desert hotel" experience that influenced him to cast his lot with outcast Dhatki people gives a poignant picture of the reality of ostracism that is the tragic plight of many in our world. Don and his new wife Nancy's choice to live and minister among these outcasts can only be understood in light of the model provided by our Lord. The responsiveness of these rejected people is a reminder of James 2:5, "Has not God chosen those who are poor in the eyes of the world to be rich in faith and to inherit the kingdom He has promised those who love Him."

The Peaks Beckon: Language Learning in Pakistan

by Don Curry

Dear Sam,

Great to hear of your decision to join in the adventure of communicating the person and love of our Lord Jesus to those of this great subcontinent. I am writing to encourage you to set high goals for yourself in language proficiency. The climb is not an easy one and it is steepest at the bottom, at the start, where one is least experienced. However the upper slopes are pure pleasure, the view tremendous. You may even find after climbing one peak that other peaks hidden from sight in the valley also beckon! I trust my own pilgrimage, from a linguistic plainsman to one who enjoys climbing and the fresh mountain air, will be of encouragement and help as you start off.

PUTTERING ABOUT IN THE VALLEY

Having a one-track mind and setting that track toward medicine, I viewed most languages as being irrelevant to my destination. This linguistic myopia was not helped by living in Western Canada where English is king with few contenders to its autocratic reign. Through international student friends I became fascinated by the diversity of their cultural tapestries, the Asian ones in particular. Yet English was our medium of communication and I saw little need for another language.

My narrow view of language was shattered by India. I arrived in my final year of medical school to work for three months in a small rural hospital in the middle of that vast, disturbing yet ever intriguing country. Rapidly my linguistic poverty became evident. Frustrated by the limitations of my monolingual state, I left, committed to learning the local language well if I should ever return.

GLIMPSES OF THE ASCENT

My time in India left its mark; I departed knowing I would return. Five years later, armed with more practical medical experience I did return, this time to work in community health on the edge of the Thar desert in the southeastern corner of Pakistan, in the province of Sindh. In a linguistically complex subcontinent I could not have chosen a province that expressed that variety more fully — the scene of numerous invasions, and the site of massive immigrations of landless laborers from the overcrowded states of Rajastan and Gujerat who were drawn to work on the colossal canal networks. Its linguistic diversity has been a challenge to missionaries over the years.

Most of these laborers were drawn from the outcast tribal Kolhis, Meghwars and Bhils so aptly renamed by Ghandi as *harijans,* which translated means God's people. (He was closer to the truth than he realized. Though rejected by men, it is especially among these tribes of the lower Sindh that God's Spirit is moving. To them, the news that God loves and accepts unconditionally is truly good news.) As the canals probed to the very edge of the vast Indus flood plain, the dry clay flatlands burst into life. Following that life came others — Muslim farmers from the populous province of Punjab, Pathan traders from villages perched on the mountain border with Afghanistan, Urdu–speaking merchants from northern India fleeing in 1947 to join the new country of Pakistan.

Into this bubbling, linguo-cultural melting pot arrived one rather green, enthusiastic young Canadian, prepared medically, but with no formal linguistic preparation. On a short stop–over in Toronto on my way out to Pakistan a student at the Toronto Institute of Linguistics procured for me a copy of *LAMP* and, sounding its praises, encouraged me to try out some of its suggestions. I arrived armed with this and little else to begin my adventure and romance with the people and the languages who call the Sindh their home.

PUSHING HIGHER

A rush of camel carts, rickshaws, buses and motorcycles and a cacophony of sounds greeted me on stepping out of the quiet compound. The last thing I wanted to do was to go into that mad bazaar and make a fool of myself with a crowd watching and snickering. I felt like turning around and spending time reading Sindhi or listening to tapes. My way would be to establish myself well in the language and then venture forth from a position of security. Yet this wretched *LAMP* book wouldn't let me sit back in peace. Its central emphasis on learning language through relationships and communicating what I had learned was a thorn in my otherwise self-satisfied side. What kept me from throwing it away or keeping it to grace a shelf in my library was the sneaking suspicion that it was right.

I kicked myself into the street and started to talk in my broken Sindhi with a few people. Some days were discouraging. Hyderabad is not a monolingual city and it reflects the linguistic variety of the province — Urdu, Punjabi, Gujerati and Pushto vie with Sindhi in the streets. I would come home sweaty, tired of being misunderstood, tired of not understanding.

But there were other days — days that I would return with buoyant spirits, encouraged by people so eager to help and overjoyed that I was learning *their* language. Most westerners they had met, if they had learned any language, had learned the national language, Urdu. I was starting from a position of weakness, yet it was my very insecurity, my obvious weakness linguistically and culturally that was my strongest asset. I had come to contribute and serve but I found I first must be served and contributed to. As friendships grew I began to learn that one of the most important gifts we can give to those we have come to help is to allow them to help us. I look back on my first year as precious in the relationships that developed as people were given the opportunity to help me.

A REFRESHING SPRING

In the course of my wanderings in the maze of streets that comprise Hyderabad's Shahi Bazaar, I came to know and appreciate the proprietor of one small bookstore. Saleem, an enterprising and active man whose store was devoted to literary works, particularly in the Sindhi language, welcomed me and encouraged me greatly in my pursuit of the "strange" sounds of his mother tongue. He took a special interest in my progress and was even more careful than my language helper in correcting and advising.

At the back of his shop, crowded around a small table that served as desk and book repository and, most importantly, a place to serve the thick sweet milky tea that is the *sine qua non* of Asian hospitality, I enjoyed some of my most stimulating encounters with Sindhi and her people — a people to whom friendship and hospitality always take precedence over even the most pressing business and who take great pride in their mother tongue and its poetry. A fascinating variety of people would drop by and it was there my friendships first started. At times I would find myself in the midst of a heated discussion on the meaning of a particular word that I had asked about. At other times I could just sit back and listen to conversation flowing around me without pressure to contribute.

Looking back, it was Saleem and his "back of the store drop-in" that, after many discouraging contacts, was a key in my language progress and a gradually deepening understanding of the Sindhi people and their ways. Keep your eyes open, Sam, for such places when you start getting out and meeting people ... places where people sit together and relax, where you can sit unobtrusively and listen — people places. They are springs of refreshment on the way, and worth a hundred grammar books.

But there are crevasses, too — opening yourself to others is not without risk. Mixed in with healthy positive relationships were others that contained their share of trouble. To some, just as in the west, friendship is looked upon as a convenient channel to further one's own ends. Often the first people to approach you will be those who are more aggressive and have their own program. I was hurt several times and it is a challenge to not become cynical and hardened, to not retreat into a shell of books and tapes, expatriate friends and long letters home. Too many have taken this route, to their own loss, and to the loss of ministry which develops only this way. Keep your eyes open for the crevasses but don't stop climbing.

LOOKING BACK

By the end of a year and a half I had made solid progress. Despite my natural reticence I had gone out and met and made some good friends. With these friendships arose many opportunities to share of the One who had called me to Pakistan and who wished Sindhis to share in His forever family. Looking back over these years of learning, of falling and picking myself up again, a few thoughts on the relational approach to language learning come to mind.

Learning a language of this subcontinent takes time. There is no instant stir–and–drink approach. My first eighteen months in full-time language learning more than paid their dividends in ministry, both medical and spiritual in the years that followed. I could talk with patients and ask about their families, their hopes and fears. I could laugh and cry with them. They became people and not merely symptoms that required a diagnosis and treatment. You, Sam, are signing up for the "duration" so be hardnosed about demands on your time and skills before you are competent in the language. Say "no" so that you may be able to say "yes" with enthusiasm down the road.

This language/culture learning approach forces us to deal with the essence of the missionary task. This essence is not found in merely being a good nurse, administrator or teacher, not even a good speaker or debater. The essence of our task is personal relationships with people as people. This involves getting involved in their lives. It involves listening as well as speaking, receiving as well as giving.

To struggle to go out into the swirling life of the bazaar from our secure haven and to become vulnerable, is to face the reality of what it means to be a missionary. For many of us it is easier to serve, to help, to teach, even to "evangelize and preach," and each of these is vitally important in our overall calling. Yet each ministry finds its fullness within the context of "to know" and "to be known."

CLIMBING HIGHER

Eighteen months after my arrival I left Hyderabad to start work in Kunri, six hours by bus and train to the east. The hospital in Kunri where I was to work, with its wards for women and children backed by the large eye ward, serves both the people of the irrigated area to the west and of the less populated but more needy desert to the east. A walk through its wards paints a picture in miniature of the tremendous cultural mosaic that is the lower Sindh. I moved into a rented flat above the main bazaar and started to work in tuberculosis control and community health while I continued part-time language learning.

Despite my increasing fluency in Sindhi and understanding of the people and their culture, as my second year slid into the third I faced an increasing identity crisis. To many, I was a Muslim. I dressed in the long shirt and baggy pants common to most men outside of cities, had a short Sindhi style beard and, most importantly, I spoke Sindhi, the language of the Muslim majority. I had been given a Sindhi Muslim name, *SANVARN KHAN*,which stuck. Most of my friends in the bazaar were Muslim. Yet it consistently was the outcast Hindu tribals, rejected by all, who were most interested in the King and His kingdom. Consistently it was to their villages we received invitations to speak of Him Who ate and drank with Samaritans and sinners, Who was no respecter of persons.

My friends in the town could not understand why I should spend time with these people. "They're unclean, they eat dead animals, they have filthy habits, ..." the list could go on. I struggled inside, my heart wanting to work with these humble, needy people, my pride holding me back. What would my Muslim friends say? I had struggled to become accepted by them but now socializing with these outcasts was jeopardizing that position. I felt torn in two directions, wanting to be a part of both worlds. Each was mutually exclusive of the other. To seek to live in both meant to deeply participate in neither.

TWO ROADS DIVERGE — A DESERT HOTEL

Silhouetted against the horizon, the dunes of the Thar desert can be seen from the hospital. Dune after dune they march their way east to the Indian border and beyond. Working in the hospital, opportunities arose to meet and talk with these desert folk, some arriving more dead than alive after a two–day journey by six–wheel–drive desert truck and camel. Later I came to know Taru, one of the first believers from his tribe. In his village far out in the desert lived a few believers, untaught, their faith struggling to survive in the milieu of animism and Hinduism that surrounded them.

I spent a week in Taru's village, seeking to encourage Taru and the other believers and checking on the progress of the well we were helping to dig. Hand dug, brick and cement reinforced, at 200 feet down they still had no water and were discouraged. As I climbed on the desert truck for the long trip back to Kunri, the conductor was friendly and we started chatting. After gear–grinding hours ploughing through the soft sand of the tortuous desert track we shuddered to a stop for tea at a small desert hotel. Three low mud walls supporting a dubious looking thatched roof and sporting a few string beds welcomed weary travellers to stretch their legs and partake of the tea bubbling on the heat hardened mud stove.

I was invited into the hotel and our conversation continued, until they heard where I had spent the week. Anger flared, "Didn't I realize they were unclean ... that they were *Bhils* ... outcasts??!" My water glass shared my contaminated state and I must pay for a new one, and no tea was available in the regular china cups. I asked if there was a cup for Bhils, and a dirty, chipped glass was pulled out of a crack in the mud wall. With a little water I washed it out and drank the tea, confirming my status to all watching as a Bhil, an outcast. Interestingly, I had just been reading from Matthew 15 and was able to share with them about Him who radically challenged the Jewish view of holiness and ate and drank with the social outcasts of His day.

I returned to the hospital an outcast in the eyes of the Sindhi people whose language I had learned. Yet I also returned freed from the burden of trying to live in two worlds. I was aware as never before of the slights that tribal people face daily. To treat and help outcasts is acceptable, even commendable, but never to eat and drink with them. My world had been chosen in that little desert hotel over a cup of tea.

THE CALL OF DISTANT PEAKS

Five years had flown by since my first arrival in Pakistan. Then, single, totally green, ready to do battle with the intricacies of the Sindhi language. Now I was returning as part of a team of two, my new wife, Nancy, joining me to work among that same tribe whose cup had declared my status some two years before. Soon after our arrival, at the invitation of the headman, we moved out to a large village near Taru, a central one for the Bhil tribe. Our primary objective was to learn their language, *Dhatki*.

Looking back over my first term in the country I saw the years spent in language and cultural acquisition as the richest and most rewarding ones of my entire stay. Language learning had not been merely a means to getting into the real work I had come to do, rather, it had been a time of fruitful ministry in the context of being a learner. It was a time when I was free to spend time with people, to develop friendships, to know and to be known. My experience in using *LAMP* to learn Sindhi made the prospect of learning this new language — unwritten, unstudied in any formal way previously — much less daunting, and even exciting.

We moved into our new home, unsure of what lay ahead. Some warned that living so far out was irresponsible, and that I, as a doctor, would soon be swamped with patients and unable to devote time to language. They were wrong. Despite the lack of a qualified medical practitioner for many miles, people continued to frequent the many local self-taught "doctors."

Perhaps the fact that we were living in a small mud house like the rest, and that I kept my medicines down to a few simple drugs gave the impression that I was not a doctor of much significance. Both from the standpoint of undisturbed time for language learning and of dealing with my pride, this was a healthy situation. In perspective I see that our status in the society is often artificially heightened by our large institutions and the financial resources we control. Real respect (which can only be given and not demanded or bought) arises out of knowledge of the people and their ways and willingness to become involved on a personal level.

Here in the village, communication of what we know is not an option, but a necessity for survival. Our "communication time" may run from 6:30 in the morning when a neighbor lady drops in to say hello until nine o'clock in the evening when the last man leaves. One of Nancy's most important communication times was with a clay water pot on her head down at the well where the women congregate in the morning. Being the new girl on the block meant quite intense interrogation at the beginning, but gradually it became a productive time to meet women other than those in our extended family. Besides that, the mile walk with 25 pounds of water on your head is great for the posture!

Living in the middle of an extended family has allowed us to enjoy and learn from the children. Initially they were pesky and yet frightened of us. Now with love and a little appropriate discipline they have become the best of friends. They also are much more ardent in correcting pronunciation mistakes than their elders.

The very simplicity of village life and its cyclic nature made language learning easier. We arrived just after the first monsoons when planting and weeding the fields occupied all their thoughts and filled their conversation. Later, harvest was followed by the marriage season. There is a time to make quilts and a time to repair your house, a time to marry and a time to arrange marriages. Vocabulary learning is thus seasonal, revolving around what everyone is doing and talking about.

Another village reality is the major pastime and favorite leisure activity of talking. In our extended family at any one time, except in the heat of the summer day, there will be several conversations going on. It is quite acceptable to invite yourself in as long as you listen before you talk. This can be somewhat frustrating for us when we are having a time of prayer or want to talk together. Yet allowing others to drop in on us is a small price to pay for sharing their world and learning from them. They have provided advice on every aspect of life, from when we should wash our hands in the morning to how to make our curries taste better and the *chapatis* rounder. Conformity even in the smallest details is demanded and we need wisdom to know when to give in and when to choose to be different.

A Christmas Story

As we look back over our last year in the village, one incident stands out in our memories: when Nancy contracted the mumps. With Christmas approaching we were eager to celebrate it with the people we had come to know and appreciate, and we had a little program planned. However, a few days before, Nancy came down with a fever and swelling and pain on the left side of her neck. The pain mounted in severity and was not controlled by the milder pain killers we had with us. Our adopted family was most solicitous and suggested all sorts of local remedies from leaf poultices to heating a wooden spoon in the fire and putting it on the painful area.

Despite all this help, she continued to get worse. We shared a rather subdued Christmas with them. Nancy was confined to bed and folks sat on the floor and on her bed as I shared the story of Him who became weak and vulnerable that we might become strong. By that night the pain had increased and Nancy was unable to sleep. At midnight I woke up Mahavo, the headman and Nancy's adopted father, and asked him for advice. He graciously pulled himself out of bed and saddled up his complaining camel.

Mahavo and I left, the temperature below freezing, to go to the nearest town for help. As we rocked along, each in our own thoughts, he started to talk with God and ask Him why He had sent us two out, only for Nancy to be so ill. He asked God to care for us for we were guests, far from home and family, his responsibility. His prayer warmed my heart despite the cold stiffness of my limbs. The phones were not working. Unable to call Kunri for help, we obtained some more powerful pain killers from a local compounder and arrived back nearly frozen by 5 am. All night Mahavo's mother and wife had stayed up with Nancy comforting her, massaging her head and neck to relieve her pain.

The next morning while I stayed with Nancy some men went out to try and hail the first desert truck. It never arrived. Finally in the late afternoon the second arrived; the first had broken down and the second was now crammed with over 180 people. We were able to squeeze Nancy onto the edge of a seat, propped up by blankets and other women. I joined the 30 or so on the roof of the cab. Before we left, Mahavo for the first time prayed in the name of Jesus. He prayed for Nancy and the long trip in an open truck through the cold desert night that faced us. Several of the men approached me to ask if I needed any financial help and two of them travelled with us to aid us. We were overwhelmed by the care and love shown by these villagers we had known only 5 months.

We finally arrived in Kunri 16 hours later, totally exhausted yet aware that something deep had happened through this event to bond us to these people. It was our weakness and vulnerability, our need of them that brought forth such an outpouring of help and concern. It was through Nancy's mumps that we first felt that we had become family.

THOUGHTS ON THE FAIRER SEX AND LANGUAGE LEARNING

Sam, you asked me about your wife, and some advice on her language learning. First and foremost, make her progress in the language just as high a priority as yours. Help out around the home and take responsibility for the children to free her for lessons and practice with tapes. Too often the husband spends long hours in the study while his wife takes care of the house and the kids. She ends up frustrated and discouraged, counting the days until furlough and hoping they won't have to return to the field. *You are a team* and it is as important for her to be fluent as for you, even if she sees her prime ministry in the home.

In a Muslim country like Pakistan, your wife will be faced with difficulty in communicating as it is not culturally appropriate for her to initiate relationships and chat with men, though men run all the stores and shops.

Rather than retreating to the traditional school approach, this calls for creative alternatives. The responsibility rests particularly on your shoulders to help make contacts for your wife. As you make friends in the bazaar you may ask them if your wife can visit their women at home. You will need to visit their homes together, you in the guest room with the men, and your wife with the women. A healthy and reasonable objective for your first term in the country is that you *both* become fluent in the language of the people.

Don't settle for less — your own long-term effectiveness and happiness rests upon this foundation.

DESERT LESSONS

I am growing to see the importance of their belief in the connection between the physical and the spiritual. In their eyes the spirit world constantly interacts with the physical. Their worldview results in an eclectic view and practice of medicine. We may disagree with their treatment, but the reality of spiritual factors in illness is beginning to be rediscovered in the west. Terms like *holistic medicine* are being used to describe a perspective that only we in the "civilized" west have lost. As I make house calls and face difficult diagnostic problems I find myself often pulled to my knees. Prayer is welcomed and appreciated by many as are the stories of Jesus' power over evil spirits and illnesses.

I have seen a major change in my concept of ministry and what my primary goal should be. I arrived trained in community health and committed to setting up programs in this area. Living in the village has made me aware of the great diversity and complexity of the present system and how much faith patients have in it. We have a local bone setter, a local eye expert, several local and well–respected *dais* or village midwives, and two or three quite famous "witch doctors"[1] known for their cure of snakebite and for skill in freeing people from evil spirits. Too easily we roll in with our money and drugs seeking to discredit these

---

[1]The English term "witch doctor" is often much too narrow to describe these people. Usually that term implies a person who is dominated by Satan and uses power for evil. But in many places these people are more like 'medicine men' — people with important knowledge of local remedies who desire to free their fellow villagers from the results of Satan's attacks. Because of their caring attitude, these people, if approached sensitively, often have the potential of becoming allies, of trusting Jesus and joining with us in truly freeing their people from the bondage of Satan. *Eds.*

"quacks" and teach people the "right" way. Yet many remedies have been tried and tested, the bone setter is very good and the young compounder is keen on learning more.

As doctors we need to live in the community for a good while before we start any program. We need to look and listen and learn, we need to start small and gradually build as understanding and acceptance grows. We need to bring the people with us, rather than seeing ourselves as pulling them up to our level. Yes they are poor, mostly illiterate, and even "backward," but they have the ability to live, thrive and even celebrate in a setting that would send most of us home in a few weeks.

We still have much to learn, Sam, and what I have shared with you should be subtitled *Notes of a traveller, destination as yet unreached.* We do not know how long we should stay in this village, how long to give them to fully understand the claims and promises of our King, Jesus. We trust we will be obedient should the cloud move on, and not look for excuses to stay should we have become too comfortable. Pray for us that we would never stop being learners — climbers aiming for that next snow-capped pinnacle that is just a bit higher.

◊

Aretta (See over) ⇨

Unlike any of our other contributors, Dick and Aretta Loving had to learn their language "monolingually," since no Awas spoke any outside language. Their learning of the Awa language was of necessity through relationships — the small highland tribe offered no alternative. Aretta has given us an arresting inside view of this process.

The Lovings raised two daughters while living in what could be described as a primitive setting. Those concerned about the welfare of their own children will welcome the perspective Aretta gives of the trustworthiness of our loving heavenly Father toward those He calls into His service.

Dick and Aretta participated in a Language/Culture Learning & Mission course that we taught in Wewak, Papua New Guinea a couple years ago. It is always good to have a few "old hands" in those courses because it adds a note of credibility and perspective for younger missionaries. The Lovings now provide regional leadership for their mission in New Guinea and they supervise the language/culture learning of the new personnel for their region.

Communicating the Gospel — Even if Your Nose is Burning

by Aretta Loving

I'll never forget that August 4th of 1959, when I crested that last mountain top and stood looking down into a valley with a couple dozen thatch–roofed huts nestling there.

My legs were aching from hours of hiking up and down steep mountain trails. We had hiked through cool jungle forest, trudged through long expanses of hot, unshaded grassland, picked our way over steep, narrow rocky precipices, waded through swirling, shady rivers, and when we drove ourselves up, up, up that last two thousand foot ascent, I was crying from fatigue. But now the sight of that village which was to be our home for the next 15 years was enough to dry my tears and cause me to momentarily forget my exhaustion.

My husband Dick, and I, as members of Wycliffe Bible Translators, had come to Papua New Guinea (then called simply New Guinea) just two months before. A few days after arriving, a co-worker had told us about a tribe known as the Awas, who were seen around the government patrol post once or twice a year. Groups of short, muscular Awa men would emerge from the jungle, heavily armed with six–foot–long bows and barbed arrows. Twine string, made of bark, braided into their short, fuzzy locks hung

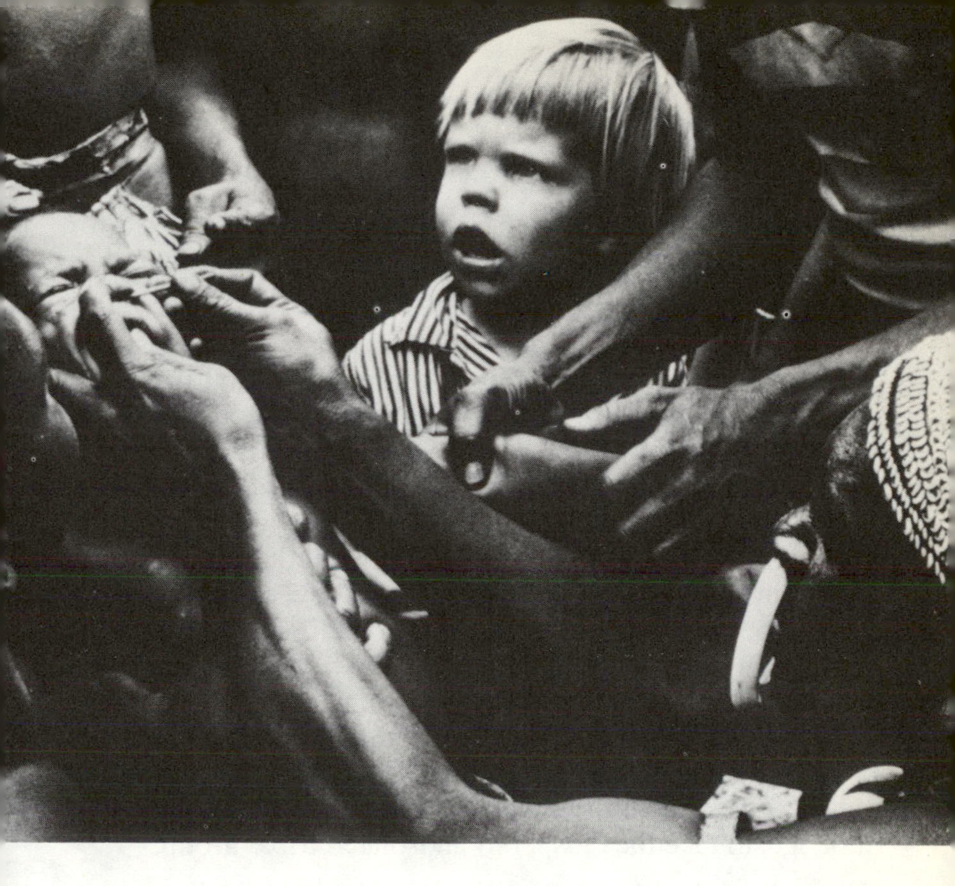

down to their waists in back, and pig tusks worn in a hole in the septum of the nose, gave them an especially ferocious look, we were told! Since they knew no Pidgin English, the trade language of New Guinea, no one from "the outside world" could communicate with them. Both Dick and I received an inner confirmation from God's Spirit that these were the people to whom He was calling us — to learn their language, their culture, and to translate the New Testament into their native tongue.

And now we were stumbling down that last winding stretch of trail, bone–tired, but elated at the thought of being there. The Awa men who had guided us through the mountains proudly and almost regally led us into their village, triumphantly bearing our few "essential" belongings. Men, women and children of the village stood silently watching the procession. Our guides put our things in a small round hut, 11 feet in diameter, then motioned for us to go inside. I smiled weakly at the watching crowd, then entered our new house.

The "furnishings" of our house consisted of one small, low bed built of poles with woven bamboo matting on it. Since the hut had no windows and the narrow doorway was only about four feet high, very little light entered. Therefore, it was only after we went to bed that night that we noticed our bed slanted drastically toward one corner. But never mind the slope, or even the fact that we'd chosen not to include a mattress as one of those few essentials — we were young, we were blissfully in our first home together as a young married couple, and above all, we were thrilled to finally be living with the people to whom God had called us. It was the moment I had looked forward to since I was thirteen, and told God I wanted to be a missionary. For Dick, it was the fulfillment of a commitment he had made in college, to take the Gospel to an isolated tribal group.

That night we slept soundly despite unfamiliar sounds — the grunting of village pigs as they scratched themselves against the sides of our hut, the loud flapping of huge bats as they winged through the village looking for food, the screeching of a chicken scurrying away from a hungry dog, and the talking that inevitably goes with stoking the fires in the chilly mountain night. Satisfied to be there at last, we slept the sleep of the exhausted.

IT'S NOT NICE TO POINT, BUT....

To communicate the Good News of Jesus Christ to this people who had never even heard His name, our first task was to begin learning their language. We had no idea Awa would be so complicated and so different from English — factors which made learning it a long, difficult process. Nevertheless as we plunged in, we very soon came to appreciate the beautiful intricacy of the Awa language, and

even more important, to appreciate the Awas as people, as real friends.

Our method of learning was, by necessity rather than choice, monolingual — we had no mutual second language through which we could communicate. Since the Awa people knew only Awa, there was no possible way to say, "In your language, how do you say ... ?" However, a compensating factor was that we had plenty of experts in the Awa language who were eager to teach us — a whole village full in fact! So we began learning from them by asking the only question we could easily pantomime: we pointed at things to ask, "What is that?" And they responded by giving the name of whatever we pointed at, even though what we were doing was totally uncultural. We later observed that people pointed with the chin and lower lip.

It was several days, well over a week in fact, before we learned to put the question into words. I was preparing some greens for our evening meal. I pointed to them, directing my "question" to a man standing on the other side of the fire. He hesitated, then turning toward the man by his side, said, *"Anepomo."*

"Tara," the other man said.

I ignored the latter word and concentrated on learning the word the first man said.

"A-ne-po-mo," I repeated carefully.

The first man leaned toward me. *"Tara!"* he said forcefully.

Now why, I wondered, did he change his mind? First he said they were *anepomo*, and now he's giving me a second name. It was hard enough to learn the first one. I tried again. *"Anepomo!"* I said, pointing to the greens, with a bit more more confidence.

The first man leaned closer still, and yelled, *"TARA! TARA! TARA!"* this time making sure I'd heard.

Finally it registered. The first man probably temporarily forgot the name of the greens, and had *asked* the man next to him, *"Anepomo?"* (What is that?) Excitedly, I began pointing at things I knew the names of, and people responded with the right name every time! I ran inside our hut, where Dick was napping — on a now leveled bed — and woke him with the exciting news.

"So you think you know how to say, 'What is that?' do you?" my skeptical husband jokingly asked. "When you tried it, did you point?" I admitted I had. "Well, I think these people are conditioned by our pointing like Pavlov's dogs were conditioned by the bell. If you pointed at something and said 'Abracadabra,' they'd come back with the right answer," Dick postulated.

"Alright, let's go try it!" I said, rising to the challenge. We went outside and I pointed to a dog and said, "Abracadabra," to one of the men. He looked at me quizzically, his eyes widened, and then he turned to someone nearby as though to say, "What's gotten into her?" I repeated the performance to several people and each time received a similar response. Then I switched to *Anepomo,* and in every case the person responded with the correct name. Dick and I had a good laugh and felt great accom-plishment at having learned how to ask our first question.

In those first weeks we spent just about every waking hour of the day and part of the night, too, with the village people. We were figuratively, and sometimes literally, "sitting at the village people's feet" and learning from them. We sat on the ground with our neighbors, listening, pointing, repeating, more listening, more repeating — using words and phrases over and over, and using what we learned to learn even more. This was sometimes fun — especially when we were able to isolate some key phrase or a question. But since so much unintelligible talk was going on around us, we sometimes felt discouraged. Listening and more listening, we knew, was one key to learning; but it often was just plain old hard work. A small cassette recorder makes this job easier today, but we've seen that with this technological improvement, the language learner can be tempted to put more emphasis on just learning the language, rather than on relating to people *while* learning the language. We found that as we learned the language through real human interaction, we were also learning the Awa customs, value system, and world view.

When conversation was directed at us, we sometimes found it advantageous to delay answering. The Awas were so eager for us to learn their language that a person would often repeat himself, giving us opportunity to hear pertinent phrases again. Once we learned to say, "Did you say?" we had a useful tool to get the Awas to say phrases over and over.

I was sitting outside with several village people around a fire when I observed an frequent drama — a pig grabbed a piece of pork lying on a banana leaf by the fire and absconded with it. Pandemonium broke loose as the people jumped up and ran yelling after the culprit. Dick and some others came running, but with everyone animatedly talking at the same time, he was unable to understand what had happened. Moving close to a group of people, I called loudly across to Dick in Awa, *"Pretty soon* a pig ate some pork." I felt foolish because I knew I was using a wrong word and the sentence was such baby–talk. Yet I repeated it, louder this time, making sure somebody heard me. It wasn't until I'd said it the third time that someone finally turned to me and condescendingly corrected me, "Say 'a while ago,' not 'pretty soon'!"

We used this technique a number of times and were amazed at the patience and insight of so many of the Awas to discern what we were attempting to say, and then to correct us. One of the most difficult constructions we learned using this method was the "contrary–to–fact," that is, "*if* something had not happened (but it did), then something else would have happened (but it didn't)." One time we gave penicillin injections to an elderly man who was dying of pneumonia, and he lived. A few weeks later I told Yera (an extremely bright young man who helped Dick with language learning and analysis), "When we were not here Old–man–Tata died."

Yera was confused. "But he's alive," he said.

"I know he's alive *now,*" I replied, "because we gave him the shots." Then I said again, "When we were not here, he died." When I had tried this feigned idiocy on some others, they never caught on, to my embarrassment. I hoped Yera would be different. Suddenly, his eyes lit up.

"Oh, you want to say, *'If* we *had not* been here, he *would have* died!'"

That was it. I asked him to repeat it, and I eagerly wrote it down. For me, the best reward of that little victory was being able to say, "If Jesus had not died for us we could not go to God's 'good place.'"

As the Awas came to know and accept us more, we spent many evening hours sitting in their smoke–filled huts talking and visiting around their fires. Every house had a fire pit. Around fires, lots of language learning kept going on. There were always two or three people, and sometimes ten or more, around our outdoor fire. We wanted to know their names, but how were we to ask? One evening, I pointed to myself and said my name, then pointed at Dick and said his name. They repeated my name, changing the first vowel, so it came out "Oretta," but Dick's name became something like "Dicky," only worse — "Edicky." (Awa words have no initial d's and no final k's, hence their inability to say "Dick.")

I was glad that they had understood that I wanted them to know our names, but no one offered to tell us *his* name. (Later we learned that Awas are embarrassed to say their own names.) Therefore, I pointed at a man and purposely

asked our now familiar question, *"Anepomo"* (**What** is that?). It worked. Someone told me the man's name, but I had a strong hunch that the meaning of *Anepomo* didn't really extend to mean "**Who** is that?" A couple nights later around the fire someone finally corrected us. "Don't say *'Anepomo,'"* he said, "Say, *'Insebo'."*

Another phrase we learned as we sat by the fire was the idiom "My–nose–is–burning." (Try to guess its meaning from the way it was used in context, as we had to.) The Awas would often clear their throats and spit into their fires. Since we all roasted corn and other food on our fire and buried sweet potatoes in the ashes to roast, I had communicated to our more regular fireside visitors my distaste for this practice. However, one evening Towaria loudly and deeply cleared his throat and — yes, you guessed it! Right into our cooking fire! I looked at him and, using my most reproachful voice, said, "Towaria!" He grinned sheepishly, slapped his chest and said, "My–nose–is–burning!"

My first thought was, "Oh, he's saying, 'I'm sorry!'" When asked what he meant, he eagerly enacted a little drama for us. He let his string bag (worn by Awa males on the shoulder) slip off onto the ground, then he got up and walked away. He stopped and felt his shoulder, then looking around he said, "My–nose–is–burning!" That context certainly didn't call for an apology, nor did "I lost it" fit the spitting–in–the–fire context. But, "I forgot" *did* fit both contexts. We filed that away in our minds, and when we put it to use in the next few days, our constant queries of our neighbors were suddenly much more suave and casual — "What is that? My–nose–is–burning."

As we learned how to ask more questions, we began to better understand the world view held by the Awas. *"Insebo?"* I'd ask one of the Awa women, jutting out my chin and sticking out my lower lip toward a man nearby.

I had asked the wrong woman for *that* man's name, as she turned out to be his wife. "Oretta," she sternly scolds me, "no woman ever says her husband's name!" She then tells me that a wife must call her husband a nickname; or if, for instance, they have a child named Mati, she may call him "Mati's father." If they have no child, she might call him something like "Umato's father," Umato being the name of their pig! (In the case of one man, people dropped the word "father" and the pig's name stuck for life.)

If the same woman were to reprimand me for calling my husband by name, I would know how to defend myself — "I don't call my husband by his name; you and I both call him *'Ani.'*" That all started when the Awas heard me call my husband "Honey." They picked it up, pronouncing it as best they could — "Ani." They found that easier to say than "Dick." At first, Dick didn't like everyone calling him "Ani," but finally he decided it was preferable to "Edicky." I explained to the village women that it was a custom in my country for women to nickname their husbands after a "certain sweet and sticky kind of food." They accepted that as just one more of our strange customs!

As we continued to ask questions, we learned more important things than just name taboos.

"Aikono?" (Where are you going?) we'd say to an Awa woman, as we saw her leaving the village with a bundle of firewood balanced on her head and food in her string bag. She might answer, "I'm going to my daughter's grave to leave sugar cane and sweet potato so she won't be hungry, and to build a fire so she won't be cold."

"Anerono?" (What are you doing?) I'd ask a mother who was rubbing her child's body with slimy, red mud. "I'm rubbing his body with mud," she'd reply. Well, that was obvious, so I should have asked, *"Anesabebo?"* (Why?)

"So his father won't beat him." The answer is enlightening, but confusing. Why would red mud keep his father from beating him? I wondered. Then I remember: the father is dead! I learn that this is the anniversary of the father's death so his child and wife are particularly vulnerable to the wrath of his ghost. The Awa believe that somehow red mud protects against ghosts beating a person and causing severe illness.

A woman crawls out of the low doorway of her hut and stands there looking at some small object in her cupped hands. Other women came to view her treasure and "Ooh" and "Aah" with her. I look at it — and it looks like only a piece of charred wood to my uninitiated eye. So I ask, *"Anepomo?"*

The answer comes back in hushed tones. *"Mera!* The shaman just blew smoke on my sick child and then rubbed him with leaves, and took this *mera* out of his insides. Now he'll get well — maybe."

In our involvement with the people we drew the line at attending any ceremonies where evil spirits or the spirits of the dead were invoked. We felt that to have done so would have been foolish and could have opened us up to attacks and oppression from the Enemy. In those days, though, as we asked questions and learned about their spiritist practices, we felt sad and frustrated that we didn't know the language well enough to tell them about Jesus who provides, protects and heals.

RAISING CHILDREN AMONG THE AWAS

As hard as we were trying to understand the Awas, we were glad when they reciprocated, and began plying us with questions too. The better we understood each other, the closer we came to our goal of becoming belongers in the Awa culture.

"Is your mother there?" they would ask, meaning "Is she alive?" "Is your older brother there? Your father?" Dick would answer, "Yes, my mother is there; and my older brother too. But my father isn't there; he died when I was a young, unmarried man."

That was a shock to the Awas. "Oh, do red people die too?" (We always were red, or pink, to the Awas, not white.)

"Yes," we'd reply, "red people die too. And we get sick. When we cut ourselves, we bleed like you do."

What a revelation that was to the Awa mind. Previously, they thought we were probably super–human; most likely, we were spirits of their ancestors.

The women were fascinated by the soles of my feet, which they acclaimed as "just like a baby's," and my long, straight hair, which was proclaimed "Beautiful — just like a pig's tail!" However, they were frustrated because they couldn't see my breasts. *"Anesabebo?"* (Why?) they would ask. They couldn't seem to understand why showing my breasts should cause "my forehead to be on fire" (embarrass me). I was scolded for what was, to them, a false sense of modesty. "Oretta," I heard more than once, "having your breasts showing isn't a thing to cause your forehead to be on fire. It's like having your nose showing."

Becoming a mother caused me to be even more accepted by the Awa women. Though I had declined their invitation to stay in the village and allow the women to help me deliver my baby down in their birth huts, I had returned to the village with my baby being carried over the trail cozily nested in a string bag like they carried their babies. And I breast–fed my baby like they did. The first time I nursed Karen outdoors a cry went out through the whole village, "Come quickly! Oretta is going to feed her baby." The sound of dozens of bare feet could be heard on the village paths as women from both the downhill and the uphill hamlets raced to watch me!

The women questioned me about my delivery. "Did you *uwo uwo* (moan)?" many asked. They were delighted to hear that I *uwo uwo*-ed like they do when they give birth.

The Awa custom of shaking hands with people they are happy to see — particularly our three–month–old Karen — presented us with a cross–cultural dilemma. Our background had conditioned us to be able to almost *see* the germs being transferred from Awa–hand to Karen–hand, then right into Karen–mouth. Dick and I resolved this frustration by asking the Awas to "shake Karen's foot," rather than her hand. To their credit, they accepted this strange request (though we're sure they never fully understood our fear of dirty hands). We'd hear insiders instructing people from other villages, "Shake our little sister's *foot,*" and you would have thought that the idea had originated with them.

Both our daughters, Karen and Treesa, look back on village life in those early years with fond memories. Neither of the girls ever hindered me from spending time with the people and learning the Awa language. To the contrary, they provided a common bond between me and the women, as well as opening up areas of conversation about "women things" like menstruation, pregnancy, childbirth, miscarriage, child–rearing discipline — and the Awa beliefs and taboos connected with these areas of life.

Almost every week day after a seven o'clock breakfast, I'd take one, or both, of the girls and we'd go to a place in the village where women with their children congregated to sit and soak up the early morning sun after a chilly Highland night. Some would be eating their breakfast — usually roasted sweet potato[1] left over from last night's

[1]Since the sweet potato is the staple food for the Awa people, we ended up translating the phrase "Jesus is the Bread of Life" by the phrase "Jesus is the ever living Sweet Potato."

meal. The generous Awas often wanted to share this with their "two little sisters," and Karen and Treesa never seemed too full to accept their offerings. Their enjoyment of cold sweet potato further endeared them to the Awas.

By about nine–thirty in the morning, people would begin to leave the village — the women and their daughters to go to their gardens or perhaps down the two-thousand-foot incline to fish in the river; the men with their dogs to go to the forest to check their traps, or to collect vine for making or repairing their garden fences, or to hunt marsupials. Most days by noon the village was fairly empty, with only the old, the sick, and a few children (mainly boys) still around. We'd then eat our noon meal; afterwards Karen and Treesa would nap; and by mid-afternoon we were ready to begin interacting with the people again.

In a thatch room completely open on one side, built as a study for me near our new large thatch home, Dick had erected a play pen of poles in the corner, and there each of our girls played before walking age. We hung a baby–seat in a tree near the house for them as well. Both enjoyed being surrounded by attentive Awa children or adults and were never fearful of any of the Awas, even those from other villages. But the white face of a stranger was another story! One day when Karen was about three years of age, one of our American co-workers walked out to spend a week with us. Karen was at the far side of the village when she arrived and seeing her, she ran screaming to the house, terrified of the white–faced lady!

Both girls quickly learned to speak Awa. One amusing incident which illustrates Treesa's language expertise was her swearing in Awa when she was three years old. More than one parent told us, "Treesa is swearing. Beat her!" Though they thus admonished us, we could tell they were amused, and perhaps even pleased, by this mastery of their language. When I asked what she had said, I was always told, "I would never repeat that! It's too terrible!"

I would reply, "She doesn't swear in English, only in Awa. *You* taught her to swear, and you teach your children too." Of course, they resolutely denied that they had done any such thing.

"Well then," I'd ask, "who *did* teach them?" They always came back with, "Well,... nobody. They just swear!"

One day I heard Treesa right outside the window and she was swearing! She was holding a kitten by the scruff of the neck, spanking it and scolding it. "You're a child from the vagina," she was telling the kitten in Awa. Somehow, I didn't have the strong emotive feel about that phrase that the Awas have, and I felt no compulsion to "beat" Treesa. I didn't even let her know that I had heard her.

When Treesa was just over three and Karen almost five, we had a one–year furlough in the USA, and by the time we returned to Papua New Guinea, both girls had lost their ability to speak Awa fluently. It was time to begin them on school correspondence courses in the village. And I felt it was important to teach them there in the morning hours when they and I were at our best. As a result, they missed out on being outside when the people were still around, so they never again became fluent in Awa. Now I regret that I didn't allow them to play with the children in the morning and teach them in the afternoons. Both girls always had a deep love for and interest in the Awas and felt a part of the work of giving them the New Testament in their own language, and they too regretted losing their fluency in the Awa language. I now recommend to new missionary couples to set their schedules so both they and their children can take advantage of the time when most of the people are in the village for interacting with them, and to schedule school work for those times when the people are normally out of the village.

Living for months at a time with two small children in an isolated village, two long, hard days' walk from the nearest medical post, was not without times of frustration and stress. Despite the close contact we all had with the Awa, none of us ever had a lice–infested head of hair — but we did get occasional attacks of malaria (even though we all religiously took our weekly prophylaxis). When we would go into our main center, stool tests often revealed that at least one of us, and sometimes all of us, had hookworm (though none of us felt any symptoms). Diarrhea was common among the Awa children, and our daughters weren't exempt either. Nevertheless, we look back and give praise to God for how He cared for and protected us.

On one occasion, when Treesa was about a year and a half old, she had a persistent case of diarrhea. After I had given her dose after dose of medication and seen no results, Dick began encouraging me to stop the medicine and together we would trust the Lord to heal her. I couldn't seem to agree with my husband; though I desperately wanted to see Treesa well, my inner turmoil kept me from being able to simply trust God to act. She grew more and more lethargic each day. One day standing by her bed, I cried out, "Lord, please, make her well!" Then I heard a clear inner voice say, "I will, if you will stop giving her medicine and trust me alone." I gave her no more, and from that point on she began to improve! In a matter of days, she was back to her happy, energetic self.

On a different occasion, Karen (our oldest daughter) was frequently waking and screaming in terror. Her eyes would be glazed and she would refuse to be comforted, pushing me away. One night as we stood by her pole–crib and saw her standing there backing away from us and screaming, I said to Dick, "The thing about this is, it's just *not* normal!" The Holy Spirit spoke softly to my heart, "Of course it's not, so why do you continue to try to treat it as though it were?" I told Dick, and we prayed, claiming our authority over the enemy. When Dick said "In the name of Jesus...," Karen suddenly relaxed against my shoulder. In the next few nights as this recurred, we would rebuke Satan and the "night terror" went away. Praise God!

A lot of young Christians today are concerned about how their children would fare on the mission field. Our children fitted into our schedules beautifully — and in their early years they actually had more of our time and attention than if we'd lived "normal" lives in our homeland. Both are proud of their unique background, and neither ever complained of having felt neglected in their growing up years, despite the fact that they sometimes spent as much as four months at a time apart from us in school at our main center. We give praise to God for His faithfulness in having kept and protected them, physically and spiritually.

MISSIONARIES: GOOD–FOR–NOTHING PEOPLE?

As I sat nursing Karen one day, Tipea, one of the young women, moved over close to to me and asked, "Oretta, have you become a worthless, good–for–nothing person?" By this time we knew their culture well enough to realize why she would ask such a question. They'd accepted us as people rather than spirits of their ancestors, but what *kind* of people were we, anyway? Who else but worthless, good–for–nothing people would "throw away" their village, their relatives, their aging parents, their gardens, their pigs — all that made life worth living — and travel day after day over the trail to a village not their own, and then spend the days just sitting and talking, rather than making gardens or tending pigs? All around, the women were sitting and watching, as though they had appointed Tipea to ask me the question they all had been wondering.

"No, Tipea," I answered, "Honey and I haven't become worthless people. We came here to tell you and your people about our 'Creator Father who is there' (Our God who is alive!). If we had not come, no one would yet be able to tell you about Him." At that point my ability in the Awa language wasn't enough to even tell them that this Creator–Father "very much wanted each one of them in His liver" — that is, loved each one of them greatly. As Tipea faced me, I felt the look in her eyes was asking me another question, "Could anything be that important? So important that a person would throw away all those things that make up life itself?" That evening as I told Dick about this strangest–of–all questions the women had asked me, we were reminded of Jesus' words in Mark 8:35, "... the person who 'throws away' his life for my sake will keep it." Later, some of those women responded to that message and realized for themselves why we were willing to "throw away" our lives by coming to live with them.

BRINGING THE GOOD NEWS OF OUR "OLDER BROTHER"

Learning the Awa language and culture by immersing ourselves as a family into village life, was a full–time job — very taxing, very demanding, but also very rewarding.

Some educated people we have talked with over the years couldn't understand why we would spend years learning the intricate tonal language of the Awas. Dick had a good answer: "Suppose someone told you he had an important message for you — however, it was in the Hungarian language rather than English. In order for you to receive that message, all you needed to do was to learn Hungarian! Would you be motivated to take on the Herculean task of learning another language just to hear what he wanted to tell you?" Even though we were surrounded by the language and culture, and we were motivated because we knew what that "important message" was, learning Awa was still difficult enough for *us*, how could we have expected a *whole tribe* of people to learn English?

When language learning hit a plateau for a week or two (as it has a way of doing!) it seemed not only difficult, but an impossible task. However, when the learning was going quickly, it was fun, exciting, and even exhilarating. But not until we knew the language well enough to be able to share the Good News about our Lord Jesus did we experience our greatest rewards — seeing people turn to Jesus one by one. Seeing over 100 people from a previously totally illiterate society learn to read and write. Completing the Awa New

Testament in 1974 and a book of 92 Old Testament stories in Awa the next year. And the crowning reward of seeing an indigenous church emerging and growing and beginning to reach out to other villages.

This process, however, took longer than we had anticipated. When we came to New Guinea in 1959 we thought that since the Gospel is such good news, when the people heard it in their own language they would quickly throw away their old heathen practices and turn to the Lord. We still strongly believe in evangelizing and discipling people in their own language, but it was just not as simple as we had first thought it would be.

As we shared the gospel, we tried to follow the principle of not speaking out against culturally–approved practices until we first knew the language well enough to discuss them and learn the reasons and motivating forces behind them. As well as learning of the Awas' fear of evil spirits and ghosts, we became aware of mothers in the birth house killing unwanted babies when instructed to do so by the fathers. We also discovered that before a husband–to–be was permitted to have his bride, his god–fathers, one–by–one, would repeatedly take the bride out briefly into the jungle at night for several weeks until she was considered "safe" for the groom.

We knew if we denounced such practices, the people would stop being open and honest with us about such things, and the practice would merely "go underground." So, as we were able, we translated parts of God's Word which speak specifically to practices which God forbids, and then let the Holy Spirit make the right application in the hearts of those who wanted to please God. Therefore, when a certain custom was discarded, it was because of what God says about it, not because we imposed our own cultural bias on the Awas.

When first trying to communicate the Gospel to the Awas, Dick was careful to get feedback as he taught, by asking them to retell what he had attempted to say. By doing this, he was able to correct any wrong messages immediately. He was often surprised at how much difference there was between what he *thought* he was saying and what they *told* him he was saying. It's one thing to be able to talk about gardens, babies, and pigs, but something else to communicate spiritual truth! He was teaching from John's gospel and when he got into the third chapter the Awas understood him to be saying, "Unless you give birth to someone, you can't go to be where God rules." Certainly not what Dick, or St. John for that matter, had in mind! Worse still, Dick didn't seem to be able to correct it. Regardless of how he tried to phrase it, the message came back to him the same. We concluded that we had tried too soon to communicate such deep spiritual truths; therefore, we changed our approach and focused on simple New Testament stories and omitted difficult parts of the narrative for which we didn't have equivalents at that time.

The day finally arrived when we were ready to begin actual translation — the Gospel of Mark! How excited we were! But the enemy wasn't about to let that milestone go unchallenged. Our main translation helper (the one Awa who had, we felt sure, become a Christian after Dick had spent months discipling and training him) suddenly left to go off to work on a coastal plantation for two years. Traumatic experiences such as this, plus the slow response of the Awas to the Gospel, were our greatest hardships — much greater than the primitive living conditions or the remoteness of our village. After we were there about four years, the Awas probably understood the facts of the Gospel better than many American churchgoers, and they could pray most impressive prayers. Yet we knew most had just added parts of the "Christian" ritual to their animistic world view and lifestyle. They were still very much afraid of death and of the ever–lurking ghosts and evil spirits. When there seemed to be little danger of getting caught, they still stole from each other and from us.

Bit by bit, though, we found the ways that God had prepared the Awas to receive His truth. During our first years in the village, it was evident to us that an Awa man's older brother was the most important person in his life. When an Awa man is accused of wrongdoing, his older brother comes and stands at his right side and answers the charges against his younger brother. If necessary, he even physically protects him from his accusers. The person who does this is called an *enei* in the Awa language, and this expression fits in beautifully for translating "advocate" in I John 2:2, "If any man sins, we have an advocate with the Father, Jesus Christ the righteous." So, to speak of Jesus being the Christians' older brother and filling the role of the *enei* as he stands by our side, answering the accusations and defending us against the attacks of the devil, is a beautiful redemptive analogy for the Awas!

By the time we left for furlough after five and a half years, Awas were reading Mark's Gospel and I John in their own language, yet we saw no change in their lives because of that. The only thing we could do at that point was pray for our Awa friends.

When we came tramping back across the mountain trail a year later, we were eager to see the villagers again, and see how the Holy Spirit had applied God's word to hearts. We were greatly disheartened, though, when we met our translation helper on the trail. He had finished his two–year stint on the coastal plantation, and now was again leaving the village for another two years.

But the next day, God demonstrated to us that He was working everything out according to His plan. We met two young Awa men on the trail whom we had taught. They excitedly told us they were going around from house to house at night, reading from Mark's Gospel, telling people that this was indeed "true talk" and admonishing them to "call on Jesus now, before a death adder bites you, or you drown in the river, or you get some big sickness and die [all very real dangers in village life]. If you call on Him now, when you die you'll go to His good garden."

As we settled into the village again, we rejoiced as we watched these two young men in action — they were no longer frightened by the thought of death; they had a definite assurance that they belonged to Jesus and would go to be with Him when they died; they wanted to please the Lord instead of just using Him to further their own ends; they had concern for their friends and relatives who still didn't know the Lord; and, their lives demonstrated a peace and joy that only knowing Jesus Christ can give. These were the signs of being born again by God's Spirit that we had waited long to see in the Awas.

These two young men became the first two "building blocks" of the Awa church. Gradually God added others, until, in time, elders and deacons were appointed and believers were going out to other villages, teaching from translated portions of God's Word in their own language.

Now when we return to visit the Awa church, we realize again the joy and fulfillment of having shared and given so many years of our lives to them in order that they might have God's Word in their own language. That joy far exceeds the frustrations and times of loneliness we sometimes experienced when we were there. And we give praise to God for the grace and strength He gave to accomplish what we felt He led us to do.

◊

Doug and Patti dropped by our office one afternoon after they had completed training at Missionary Internship. We talked about bonding, relationships, language learning and ministry strategies. Later, Doug wrote from the field saying that one of the most important things that had been shared with them that afternoon was the concept that God was taking them to their country and that God had already gotten there first. Doug and Patti have made it a goal to seek to discover how God got there first and how He has been preparing the people for Himself, and they have laid aside other ministry agendas in order to be with the people, to learn from them, and to deeply understand their culture — and to wait on God.

We find it interesting to contrast the cultural experiences and insights gained during the Child's first year with the relative lack of similar experiences which was typical of the students in the missionary language school we worked at a number of years ago. Even if community language learning were slower than school learning (which it seldom is), all the cultural and relationship benefits of learning with people would still make it more than worthwhile.

Doug and Patti went to their middle-East country, where they had no prior contacts and "plunged right in." In their contribution, they have given us a fascinating picture of their first year of language learning and ministry.

Be With People — Wait on God

by

Doug (& Patti) Magnuson

Were we really in the 20th century, I wondered, as we entered the Muslim cemetery. Or were we back in the time of Mohammed or even Abraham?

We passed through the midst of white coffins, above ground in typical Muslim fashion. The crowd we were in moved with a flourish of rhythmic drumming and vigorous singing toward the tomb of the local *uli* or *marabout,* a holy man now long dead but still thought to be able to impart blessing to sincere seekers. We were in a circumcision procession, visiting the saint to seek God's blessing on this most important event which marks a boy's entrance to the community of men and, more significantly, of believers.

Entering the tomb complex, we stepped forcefully into another world. Time stopped, as we stooped and squeezed one by one into the tiny well room, whose water each one drank solemnly in his turn for its *baraka* or blessing. We then entered the sacred place where the marabout's body lies, while candles were lit and placed on his coffin, and unuttered prayers were offered. We stepped back into the central courtyard to fervent drumming, singing, and dancing. The air was thick with the tradition of practices and beliefs passed down over long-past generations.

We left the tomb and proceeded back to the house of the boy's grandmother, everyone now more subdued. Dusk was settling gently on the town. Crowds gathered in the narrow streets to investigate the source of excitement. The small courtyard of the house was running over with people and an atmosphere of anticipation. Children peered down from rooftops — yet-uncircumcised boys pondering when their turn would come? It seemed we were in Bible times.

This was not the rare experience of an anthropological field worker. No, it might also belong to anybody open to language learning through relationships with people.

Entry: Diving Into the People's Language

Ours is at least a three-language country. In addition to colloquial Arabic, which everyone speaks, most people at least in the cities and towns understand classical Arabic, and speak French to some degree due to French colonization. With the country's virtual bilingualism in French, many Americans coming here take time out to learn French or even classical Arabic beforehand, thinking it will help them make the adjustment to life here. We had been set on such a course, but after talking to such advocates of incarnational ministry as Dwight Gradin of Missionary Internship, Greg Livingstone of Frontiers, and Tom and Betty Sue Brewster, we came to the conclusion that learning French first would be doing it backwards. So we decided to take the "cold plunge" — straight into colloquial Arabic.

The rewards have been tremendous. Taking the plunge has been harder perhaps in the short run, but easier in the long run. Not knowing any language when we came, there were times we simply could not do what we needed to do, and times when we could not express what we wanted to say to our friends. But by being forced to use Arabic all the time, we learned it faster than we would have had we had French to fall back on, especially since French is automatically spoken to any foreigners. We *constantly* had to explain, "We don't speak French, only Arabic."

The people quickly brighten up when we we speak to them in Arabic, and they compliment us generously for our wisdom in learning Arabic first. There is nothing quite so satisfying as hearing the delighted exclamations of those who claim we are the first foreigners they have met who speak Arabic, and carry on as if it were the greatest thing they've ever seen.

Together with our attitude toward language learning, taking the cold plunge promoted the process of "bonding" with the people. We did not know anyone in the country when we came, and so we were not met at the port, taken to an American home, or toured around.

As we stepped off our boat into the smothering heat, anxiety attacked. This anxiety, however, turned out to be for the good. We were made much more aware of our dependence on God, in every way. First, we had to make it through customs with no language ability, and find our way into Sarabia City for a place to stay. Then, as we got out onto the streets, we had to trust God for people to meet and relate to. Not having any initial contacts, we came to the task with absolutely nothing to offer, and had to utterly rely on our Heavenly Father. I don't know of anything which brings more joy or excitement than calling to God out of complete poverty, and seeing Him provide.

An important result of taking the cold plunge was being forced from the very first day to be out among the local people. Being committed to total immersion, we chose as our first quarters a small no-star hotel on a busy shopping street in downtown Sarabia City. From there we began to get out and meet people.

During those first weeks the two of us went out together into the community. Day after day we walked the crowded streets of modern Sarabia City and the narrow walkways of the busy *Medina* (the centuries-old section of town), talking mainly with shopkeepers and vendors, but also people in the street, when they started conversations with us. Whenever we met someone who knew some English, we would ask how to say something new — whatever we needed most. At first, it was "Hello and good-bye," then "I want to learn Arabic," then "What do you call that?" and so on. Our strategy was: *Learn the little bit we need most right now, and use it as much as possible.* I should point out that neither Patti nor I are the kind of person who freely makes friends with people on the streets. In the U.S., you just don't *do* that sort of thing. But here, people are very friendly toward foreigners, and they often initiate the conversation.

FEELING AT HOME

An important objective in our learning strategy was to live with a native family. To find an amenable family, we supposed we should meet all the people we could. Our supposition turned out to be right on target, because we later found that in this culture, everything is accomplished through contacts — that is, friends who have friends, who have friends.... But while we were waiting on this objective, the Lord did bless us with some experiences in relationship that met our needs beautifully.

During the first two months we were here, we developed many relationships with shopkeepers, as well as two deeper relationships which in many ways kept us going in this initial and sometimes difficult period. One was with Abdul, a handsome, sportive young man with a ready smile and a slight stutter, whom we met one night on a park bench during our first week in Sarabia City.

"Aasslãma, Aasslãma" (Hello, hello), we said to him, recognizing him as a man we had briefly encountered the day before on a busy street.

"Shnuwwa hwãlik? " (How are you?)

On recognizing us, his face broke into a smile. *"Lãbãs, lãbãs "* (Fine), he returned with surprise.

"Titkallimush bilAarbi?" (Do you speak Arabic?) With excitement, he started rattling off questions at us that we couldn't comprehend. Good thing we had learned how to stop him.

"Nitkallimu shwayya bark bilAarbi" (We only speak a little Arabic), I interjected.

"Ah, *Parlez-vous Francais?"*

"No,..."

"You speak English!" he said with certainty.

"Yes — but we'd like to learn Arabic," Patti replied.

"Good, good! Where ... you are from?" he asked. We began to learn about each other, using our few Arabic phrases and his sketchy English. Suddenly Abdul stood up.

"Come! Come!" he said enthusiastically.

"Where are we going?"

"We will have coffee," he said, waiting for us to follow.

The men here just about live in the cafes, which abound everywhere. But this evening, Abdul could not find one to his liking, and he invited us to go with him to his home. We were elated! We went to their small home in the medina, met his mother, grandmother, brother, and two sisters, and spent the evening sitting with them, interacting by facial expressions and gestures and through Abdul's English. That night I wrote in my journal:

> I kept thinking what a privilege for us to be in a home, not even one week into our stay. God at work. I can scarcely contain myself for wanting to sing His praises and wanting to get out again and see what He might do.

This turned out to be "home" for us for a long time, as we spent many evenings there, feeling extremely thankful to God for His provision.

Our other significant early relationship began to develop when we stopped one sweltering summer afternoon to cool ourselves off with some ice cream at a local *Patisserie.* Omar, the scooper, was a lively, jolly guy about our age (late 20's). He immediately began a lively conversation with us, despite the fact that we had no more than 20 words in common. We hit it off, and he turned out to be our best language helper. We never had trouble communicating, due to his friendliness and his ingenuity in expressing himself and understanding us. He assigned himself as our "helper," and would spend time with us every day, sometimes for hours on end.

One day in particular we'll always remember. Omar took us to a lovely park, which was to become a favorite language learning spot for us. As we sat on the grass, he heartily began pointing to his elbow, shoulder, hand, knee, foot, and for each one he would declare its Arabic name, and exhort us to mimic him.

Then he started tugging at different pieces of clothing. *"Suriyya,"* he forcefully pronounced, as he tugged at his shirt. *"Sandal,"* he declared, holding his sandal in the air. We dutifully did our best to make our mouths make the same sounds. When he ran out of clothes, he started on colors, and when he ran out of colors, he started giving us orders in Arabic. "Sit down! Stand up! Walk! Turn around!", he ordered, straining our comprehension capacity. *Then,* he randomly pointed out everything we had learned. One by one, he would point at an object, and say, "Speak Arabic!" If we botched our pronunciation, he'd say it again, in his best "school teacher" voice. Times like this were delightful learning experiences, and to this day I owe my knowledge of items of clothing, body parts, colors, and many basic commands to Omar.

It was just our second week in Sarabia City when Omar asked us one day to meet him at the Patisserie. We showed up, having no clue about what we were doing. Much to our surprise, we found ourselves on a train, and then a bus, finally to discover we were visiting his sister's house. Soon we were sitting in their humble little living room being looked over by a steady stream of neighbors as they learned of our arrival. The visit lasted three days and two nights in this tiny two-room home, even though we had brought nothing at all with us — no toothbrush, no razor, no pajamas, not even a contact lens case (two glasses of water managed to hold my precious lenses). Throughout the time, we felt overwhelmed with gratefulness to God for this opportunity, and for the special warmth that comes from having friends in a new place.

I wrote in my journal:

> All the time we were there we had one extended language learning time. Omar and Najet teaching us 'Give me. Take. I see ...' It seemed hundreds of words, from cup to soda, food, mountain, swim, beach, sand, pots and pans, empty, full, body parts, clothing, animals, etc. I kept agreeing with Brewsters, this *is* the most enjoyable setting for learning a language — in the context of real-life situations.

We are now many months and many experiences down the road. Throughout our time here, lessons from those first few weeks have stuck with us. We learned we have to be totally flexible, ready to do anything at any time with anyone. This flexibility often means setting aside our comfort and our schedule — such as when we took our surprise three-day trip to the home of Omar's sister, or later in that same tiny house when we were sleeping shoulder to shoulder on the floor with 30 other people.

Sometimes flexibility means being ready to try new things — such as breakfast when we were fed goat's milk that had been in the goat minutes before. But the rewards are good experiences, excellent learning opportunities, and growing both in the Lord and in cultural sensitivity.

LANGUAGE LEARNING: CONTACT OR CLASSROOM?

Our early experiences have taught us that language is best and most enjoyably learned through relationship with the local people. Although God has blessed us with a number of friends, we have not had success in finding language helpers to work with on a regular basis, for learning new phrases and practicing pronunciation and comprehension. Our solution has been to use *all* of our contacts as helpers, wherever we may meet them. And, thanks to the cassette recorder, the effectiveness of the help we do get is multiplied many times. When they are able, we have our friends tape dialogues and stories, and then we are able to listen to our helpers anytime, any place.

As Americans, we found we have a strong tendency to be sucked into a classroom approach (especially someone like myself, who has spent more than twenty years behind a desk.) I admit I miss the set schedule of the classroom. I have sometimes found it difficult to rise in the morning with a full day open before me with no set schedule. How much easier it is to relax and let someone else set the schedule — the "be at class by eight o'clock" routine.

We have used classroom resources from time to time. A school does have its usefulness. After spending six weeks on the streets, we took a 6-week, four-hour per day course at a language school in Sarabia City just as a resource, for input and stimulus. The teacher was for us a helper. In class, the teacher spoke only Arabic, with little grammatical explanation. We determined to spend our time outside of class not "studying" (trying to learn dialogues or vocabulary) but rather being with people. We didn't try to learn everything, as a classroom approach dictates, but concentrated on what we needed to know to communicate.

All the praises we have for relationship-oriented or "total immersion" language learning notwithstanding, this approach brings with it some difficulties. It is draining to learn language out with the people. It takes a lot of energy to relate to people from a different culture, and with language skills that just barely begin to probe the thoughts and feelings below the outer layer of conversation.

When you're with people, you're also asking for relationship problems — the kind of problems that often leave you at a loss for words in English, let alone rudimentary Arabic. For example, what do you do when your new friends turn out to be very possessive, and don't want you to have other friends? Or when your friends help you look for an apartment with the expectation that, when they find a place which *they* know is "just right" for you, you will automatically take it.

Finally, with people-based language learning, there's no way to avoid sometimes feeling vulnerable and foolish. We are educated American adults, accustomed to being respected and respectable, and it is hard to be out all day bumbling along in a language we do not speak well. It makes it very tempting to retreat to the classroom, wait until all our language problems are behind us, and on that mythical day emerge into the world talking like a native.

LANGUAGE LEARNING THROUGH RELATIONSHIPS PAYS OFF

We have found that these difficulties, though, are more than overcome by the great advantages of learning through relationships. For one thing, our *motivation* is much higher when we're striving to communicate with a friend, than when the teacher demands us to randomly substitute a new subject noun and make agreement in the verb and predicate adjective. When I am with people, I *want* to communicate. As I follow the principle of getting what I most need *now,* and then using it, I'm focussing on what is essential to me and therefore of great interest. I still remember learning the word for "between." People always asked where we are from, and we told them — Rhode Island. But no one had ever heard of it, so I had to explain that it is *between* Boston and New York. I learned it, and quickly, because I *needed* it.

The days are still vivid in my mind when I began to focus on Arabic words like believing, following, forgiveness and obeying. I was continually peppered with questions about whether I believed in God, whether I was a Muslim, and so on, and I needed to have answers. As soon as I learned these words I had an opportunity to use them immediately.

The next friend I made asked me, "So you're learning Arabic? Are you a Muslim?" I was able to answer him, "I submitted my life to Jesus, and I follow him." I wanted to tell him so much more about my life in Jesus, but I lacked the vocabulary. I jotted down four or five words I needed but did not know. I was so eager to learn them, I rushed home to find them in my Arabic New Testament, went over them several times, and returned to my friend the next day to continue the conversation. Never in all my years of school have I been so motivated to learn — all because I needed new words to communicate with people.

Furthermore, learning through relationships has brought certain enlightening *cultural experiences* our way that I wouldn't trade for the world's best classroom experience. As we have been out making friends, God has blessed us with an abundance of adventures.

Friends have taken us to weddings, the public baths (men and women go at separate times), the beach, the beauty parlor, and even to view the tomb of a *marabout,* or saint. Over half a dozen families have extended to us the hospitality of an overnight stay, and many more have insisted that we come for a meal.

People, their environment, and their language, made indelible images on our minds and hearts. A woman shared a breathtaking panorama with us on the coast. As we stood with Thouraya in the swirling breezes atop the walls of an old mountain-top fort, she made a wide sweep of her arm, urging us to soak in the beauty of her country. The sea, the mountains, the bustling village below were resplendent in a brilliant tropical sun. You can bet we never forgot the phrase she taught us that day — "This is a beautiful view." We had intended to camp on the seashore, and had met Thouraya on the beach. When she learned we were in a tent, she insisted we come and stay with her family in the village. We spent two days with them.

On a trip through the southern part of the country, we learned the verb "to ride," when we ourselves mounted camels that lurched across the desert sands. Similarly, when we learned the word for oasis, *"wãha,"* it was positively brimming with meaning for us — we were walking down a road that plied its way through a beautiful oasis, when a farmhand approached and befriended us.

"We love this place," we told him.

"Isn't it beautiful," he replied, "I work here, on a farm." He shared with us what he did from day to day in his job, and his stories filled our image of *wãha* with life.

Several experiences have reaffirmed for us that people really do help people who are in need. Once, on a trip we pulled into a station after midnight and found everything closed. A friendly young man we met en route took us home with him. A few days later we arrived in a small town on the edge of the desert and headed for the police station to ask where we could put up our tent. "We won't let you put it up anywhere around here," an officer told us, "because of the scorpions. Too dangerous." A cleaning man in the station overheard, and he invited us to his home — a very poor place, but he and his wife overwhelmed us with their generous hospitality for the next two nights.

Experiences like these have encouraged us to go out of our way to make ourselves dependent on our local friends instead of on foreigners. Friends have lent us (or helped us build) furniture (we brought none with us), have helped us mail packages at the post office, have driven us to the airport, have helped us buy groceries and then come over to teach us how to prepare local food their way. Their help has given us a feeling of security and being cared for in a foreign land, has given our friends the satisfaction of reaching out to people in need (us!), and has strengthened the bonds between us.

What a thrill to see God at work, even in the process of our language learning! Learning through relationships has facilitated and generated many ministry opportunities. Truely, "language learning *is* communication, *is* ministry."

Conversation on my language learning route frequently turns to opportunities to "give an answer for the hope that is in us." I am asked nearly every day: Are you a Muslim? Do you pray? Do you read the Qur'an? Do you hold to God? Contrary to the popular belief that it is difficult to share one's faith in Muslim lands, we find it hard to avoid. Unlike America, people here *want* to talk about God, and we often find ourselves faced with wide open doors for speaking of God's work in our lives — doors opened by our being out talking with people.

Passing conversations often turn into deep ongoing discussions. One of my best friendships is with an olivewood craftsman by the name of Jamel. I started dropping in on his shop, and one day he asked me what I believe. This began months of deep discussions which continue to this day. When we started our dialogue, my Arabic was not sufficient to answer all of his questions. Even so, Jamel has come very close to professing faith in Christ, because my language ability *was* adequate to explain in rudimentary form my own faith, and adequate to build the relationship between us to the point where he felt he could ask me the deepest questions of his heart.

As well as this "ordinary" sort of Muslim, I have also had contact with several members of a Muslim missionary movement. I met my first friend from this zealous group on the basketball court. After he looked over my game from the sidelines, he initiated a conversation and volunteered to help me with my Arabic. A relationship was born. I spent hours with a couple of the fellows in this group, discussing their faith and mine. My vocabulary has grown because of these sessions. This has helped me tremendously in talking about my faith. It has also allowed me to learn first-hand what Islam is to practicing Muslims, and how they conceptualize their faith. This has proven extremely valuable in talking with other Muslims. For example, as we discuss man's standing before God and how to be right with Him I am able to relate to their ideas of sin, the basis for forgiveness and salvation, and so on.

As I have come to know these fervently Muslim peers of mine, I have come to believe that God might raise up an apostle Paul out of this group — one whose great zeal and ability to evangelize people would, through conversion, be turned to work mightily for the cause of the Gospel here.

I've been deeply impressed by the conviction of Greg Livingstone that the Church has not seen a great harvest from the Muslim world because it has done so little sowing.

We have made it our goal from the first day of our language learning, to spend as many hours as possible with

Muslims, sowing in order that God might bring about a great harvest here. Language learning time is time for contact with people — exactly what ministry demands.

Learning as a Woman In the Islamic World

I don't mean to imply that we have not had our share of struggles. Our first objective, staying with a local family, eluded us — we stayed in a hotel for two months while looking for a family. We began to realize this might not be possible for a couple, since most families are large and do not have an extra room. So, we started looking for a place of our own to rent.

We found one, but it turned out to be in an area where people seemed to keep to themselves and have little contact with neighbors. Patti found this situation difficult for language learning. I can walk the streets to meet people and practice my Arabic, but she cannot. The only feasible learning strategy for a woman here is to get into networks of relationships, and that happens most easily in a neighborhood. Although our landlady, her daughter, and their two live-in maids talked with Patti nearly every day, we still were not satisfied.

The best relational and language learning experiences for Patti were those weekend-long wedding or circumcision celebrations we were invited to. These gave us a taste of life in a community where women know each other and spend time together, and convinced us that the best learning strategy for Patti would be for us to live in an area where she could have this kind of relationship.

Finally, after nearly two years of praying and searching (and working on language in spite of the difficulties of our living situation), God opened up such a place for us. We're now living in a neighborhood a short distance outside of

Sarabia City. We live with a family which includes a mother, grandmother, and four daughters. In addition to these, Patti has dozens of friendly neighbor women close at hand. Now, besides language practice in large doses, she is able to experience what life is really like for women.

BE WITH PEOPLE, WAIT ON GOD

Our way of learning and ministering boils down to a few enjoyable practices: being with people as much as possible; constantly emphasizing to our friends our desire to learn, being flexible, always ready for anything; enjoying life here, the people, food and customs; and most importantly, expecting that God will do great things as a result.

These past two years have probably been the most learning-filled time of our lives. It has been a thrilling experience to be led by God to step out, leave our friends and our secure known way of living, to plunge into life in another world.

Nothing is more overwhelming and exhilarating than to trust God as we attempt to adjust to life in a new place, to come to understand people and learn their language. We look back with a sense of satisfaction, and forward with an even greater sense of expectancy, eager to see how God will lead us next.

◊

Jeanette has served a term in Senegal, West Africa, and learned both French and Senegalese. Here she shares with us some of her feelings, in poetic style. ***(For more of her poetry see pages 163 and 188.)***

Calls

by Jeanette Chaffee

Calls,
recorded, loud prayer calls
from the white-stoned mosque minaret
I heard walking home tonight
at dusk.
Chanting, repeating the word
"Mohammed…Mohammed,"
as an incantation.

Let it someday be
Your name, Jesus!
Your name …
which is above all others.

Mickey and Joyce Smith have discovered a remarkable "redemptive analogy" in the classical alphabet of the Javanese people. This, and other analogies they are finding (they call them "footprints of God"), have been discovered because the Smiths have gotten deeply involved in the heart language of the Javanese people.

In their chapter, the Smiths recount their pilgrimage from English through the Amharic, Oromo, Armenian, Spanish, Indonesian and Javanese languages. The progression of their methodologies and attitudes extends from language school for Amharic and Oromo to the self-directed learning of Javanese.

As they follow Jesus they have recently been led into a further significant step of involvement — "moving up the mountain" to the village of Candi Baru. Before the move, they wrote us: "For however long and for whatever purpose God might design, we are off to the mountain with a warm blanket, a cook pot, a plastic table cloth, a pressure lantern and high hopes." In a later letter they wrote, "We feel like people who are almost starting all over again. The folks at Candi Baru have been very gracious and eager about our involvement there."

Joyce and Mick minister with their two very special teenage children, Susan and Mike.

Searching for Footprints of God in Rural Java

By Mickey and Joyce Smith

A pilgrimage through six languages has enabled us to begin to see that our task is to immerse ourselves deeply enough in the lives of Javanese villagers to recognize the footprints of God, and then help our Javanese friends see the One who made these footprints, and where they lead. Here we reflect on our journey in progress.

FROM THERE TO HERE IN SIX EASY LANGUAGES

ETHIOPIA — AMHARIC AND OROMO

• **Mick** • When we arrived in Ethiopia in January, 1974, we enrolled for two semesters in an inter–mission language school in Addis Ababa. There I studied Amharic, the national language of Ethiopia, as I would soon be supervising Haro mission station's elementary school, clinic, air strip, 15 employees and two mules. A year later, when I was done with language school and ready to start serving the Lord, I found Amharic to be just the right language … as long as I stayed on the mission compound! As soon as I stepped off the compound, I sank well above my ears and mouth in a sea of Oromo villagers, 98% of whom were non-literate and spoke little or no Amharic.

◊ ***Joyce*** ◊ I was encouraged to study Oromo in language school since my work would be largely with village ladies who spoke only Oromo. Few written materials were available in Oromo and my one–semester course was in a slightly different type of Oromo from what I later met at Haro. When we moved out to the station, I continued to have an Oromo language helper come often.

The times I visited ladies in surrounding villages or went to the market were both satisfying in one sense and frustrating in another. I enjoyed the little bits of progress in communicating, but was overwhelmed by what I *didn't* know. My involvement in spinning cotton or trying to learn to cook the local spiced stew and sour bread were the most successful language times and resulted in friendships. However, my mission compound duties and the comfortableness of handling the familiar world *inside* my house, rather than the unfamiliar world outside, resulted in my off-compound relationships and activities being rather few. However, in contrast to Mick's experience I did have the satisfaction of being able to communicate a little in the language of the Haro area.

• **Mick** • Imagine my thrill on our first Sunday at Haro. About one hundred and ten people were packed into a round mud hut hoping to learn more about God's Way. They had to endure my 15–minute sermon that stretched to forty minutes as my young interpreter did his best to tell the folks in Oromo what I would like to have told them myself if I could. And how did I handle the turmoil that erupted during the prayer time at the end of the service when an inquirer manifested demon possession? I didn't! I added to the chaos by trying to find a corner to hide in — tough to do in a round house! Local elders cast out the demon in Jesus' Name. I wouldn't have known what they were saying even if I had been close enough to hear. They were speaking in Oromo! After a year of sweating through lessons to become conversant in Amharic, I was still an outsider.

That frustration grew over the remaining two years before the Marxist revolution halted our ministry in

Ethiopia. Shortly before leaving the country, I attended a 10–day language seminar led by Dr. Don Larson which gave perhaps the first positive, practical direction, and insight into some of the turmoil I felt as an outsider trying to tell the good news. By the time our mission was forced out of Ethiopia, I was determined that if God allowed me another cross-cultural ministry, I would make learning to speak the local language a top priority.

PASADENA — ARMENIAN AND SPANISH

• **Mick** • A two–week intensive course in Language/Culture Learning & Mission with Tom and Betty Sue Brewster at Fuller Seminary in Pasadena doesn't sound all that threatening. And it isn't, as long as you don't venture outside the classroom — but that's not an option. The challenge was those first few afternoons of pavement–pounding all over Pasadena looking for someone who would be willing to help us learn to speak their language — in two weeks! "Fat chance!" I thought.

But I was surprised at how quickly God provided someone to give time every afternoon for two weeks as I learned to say things like, "Hello, I'm learning to speak Armenian. That's all I can say. Good–bye."

The frustrations we logged in Ethiopia prepared us to learn what God had for us in Pasadena. The Lord used the course to teach us *skills* of relating and language learning that would help us become belongers. And He also opened our eyes to the reality that our missionary task is not just to bring the Good News, but to *be* good news to the people to whom God sends us. We began to realize that if we made *knowing people* our business, we could much more naturally understand and fit into their world, earning a position from which we could legitimately share the gospel.

We learned that a *commitment* of the will is essential for those who want to be good news to people of a new culture.

◊ ***Joyce*** ◊ The Pasadena experience helped me be hopeful rather than dreading the language learning. The practical aspects of listening skills, learning to use the tape recorder to set up various types of drills and learning questions to ask to gain needed information all helped me see language learning in the realm of the possible rather than impossible. I found that the skills helped me relax in the process. I learned to focus on using the little bit of Spanish I *did* know rather than to be overwhelmed by what I didn't know. It was freeing. I still hadn't quite caught the emphasis on relationships, but I did make steps in this direction as I delved into the cultural knowledge of the people.

INDONESIA — INDONESIAN AND JAVANESE

• **Mick** • It was midnight when we received our long awaited phone call informing us that our visas to Indonesia were granted. Our chance to become a part of the rural Javanese life in Central Java was about to become a reality.

Bahasa Indonesia is the national language, so our first six months were spent in language study in Bandung, West Java. We moved temporarily into an Indonesian community in a wealthy section of town near the language school to house–sit a two–story, nicely furnished, fenced-in house for several weeks. We made regular visits outside our doors, but discovered that the Japanese business man next door and the busy Chinese–Indonesian banker across the street couldn't be of much help to us in our attempt to relate to local Indonesian people.

We asked the Lord to help us find housing in a more typical Indonesian community. And He did — a little house in a lower–middle–class community off a main road. We had much closer contact with our neighbors than we had really anticipated. Our bedroom wall joined that of the house next door. Our front door was four meters from our neighbor's. A loudspeaker from the neighborhood mosque blared at full volume five times a day. Chickens and noisy kids by day, rats dancing in the attic at night, and floods inside the house all said in a taunting way, "So *this* is what it means to belong!"

Once He got our attention, God enabled us to begin to look beyond the uncomfortable sounds, sights, and feelings to see our neighbors. As we pursued relationships outside our front door, things took on a better perspective. Soon we were included in community happenings — birthday parties, funerals, circumcision parties, events at the local mosque. These things left such deep impressions that even long after we left that community for our work in Central Java, we returned as a family to visit friends there.

After seven months in Bandung, we moved to Boyolali, a small town in Central Java at the foot of Mt. Merapi and near the cities of Solo and Yogyakarta, the centers of Javanese culture. Using Indonesian as our medium, we plunged into the study of Javanese. Because our ministry objective was to plant churches in the countryside, I regularly spent time with villagers. Joyce concentrated on becoming part of our neighborhood in town.

◊ ***Joyce*** ◊ God blessed us with a unique neighborhood. Unlike a lot of city neighborhoods, our neighborhood was a closely–knit group that did many things together.

I really struggled during those first few months of switching languages. For a while I could speak neither Indonesian nor Javanese without nervously mixing the two. Since I knew I needed Javanese to reach my target group I pressed on, sacrificing the Indonesian. Eventually it sorted itself out and now I can use both, but the negative factor of switching to another new language, only a few months after starting the first, was a stress factor that should probably be taken into consideration by most language learners.

• **Mick** • When our five months of full–time language learning in Javanese were over, we gradually assumed ministry responsibilities in the villages. According to the 1980 census, only 2.5% of Java's residents are Christians. Though these figures may be too low, the truth remains that few Javanese call Jesus "Lord," and 90% profess Islam. There is a strong Islamic current present among rural Javanese — Arabic prayers are chanted at circumcisions, weddings, and funerals. But many people in the rural areas, though registered as Muslim, hold fast to what some consider to be the true religion of Java — a system of animistic beliefs and practices that predate the influence on Java of Hinduism, Buddhism and Islam, but now is a mosaic, blending elements of all three.

FOOTPRINTS OF GOD

• **Mick** • As we pressed on in learning about the world of Javanese villagers, we began to realize that God had been here before us. His "footprints" are still visible in the lore, traditions, and facts of life that hold the rural Javanese village world together. Dr. Norris's article "God and the gods: Expect Footprints,"[1] helped clarify for me the concept of God's work in other belief systems. The following summary was particularly helpful:

> If one takes scripture with great seriousness as the paradigm for mission, then it leads the way toward 'legitimate borrowing' and viewing the 'Gospel as fulfillment.' ... The Christian borrows because God has made Himself known in various ways. ... Scripture does not see the approaches of borrowing and fulfilling as ones in which the revelation of God to Israel and in Jesus Christ is 'on a par with other

[1]Dr. Fredrick Norris, "God and the Gods: Expect Footprints," (p. 55-69) in *Unto The Uttermost,* Doug Priest, Jr., Editor (William Carey Library, Pasadena), 1984.

> religions.' What it does insist upon is the ultimacy of God's self–disclosure in Jesus Christ and the fact that in each place, in each culture, in every religion we should expect some footprints of God Himself. (p.66)

What a liberation! We wouldn't have to bring a new God to the people at all. He had *already* walked among them. But His footprints have been blurred by time and by the erosive effect of beliefs that have swept over this island in the past 2,000 years. Praise God, we would be able, in part, to start from Javanese beliefs and practices to show that the true meaning of the *slamet* (well–being) that Javanese seek is found in Jesus (the "Slamet Specialist"). Jesus guided the men on the Emmaus road to examine what they already knew, the Old Testament Scriptures, to see the truth about the Christ. Paul did the same with Jews in the synagogues around Asia minor, and used the same principle in speaking of the unknown God in Athens. Our job is to help the rural Javanese follow the footprints that God has left around them, so that they too can find The Way.

That's it! Our task was to immerse ourselves deeply enough in the lives of Javanese villagers to recognize the footprints of God. Then we could help our Javanese friends discover Who made these footprints, and where they lead.

AJI SAKA: THROUGH A GLASS DARKLY

A major factor that helped launch our search for God's footprints was the work of a Javanese Christian, Tjokrosentono, who published a small Javanese booklet in 1970 entitled *Wedaring Tjarakan.*[2] It contains a fascinating

[2]Tjokrosentono, *Wedaring Tjarakan,* (Badan Penerbit Kristen, Jakarta), 1970. [The Smiths have also published a more detailed account of this story and its use as a redemptive analogy -- see "Aji Saka: An Eyeopener for the Rural Javanese," in *Unto the Uttermost,* (ibid) pp. 216-228.]

analysis of the well–known tale of Aji Saka, folk hero and legendary creator of the ancient Javanese alphabet.

THE LEGEND OF AN ANCIENT KINGDOM: Long ago one of Java's many kingdoms was ruled by a wicked giant named *Dewatacengkar* who horribly oppressed his subjects, even devouring one of them daily. Almighty God noted the plight of his (Javanese) people and sent a young man named *Aji Saka* to deliver them. Aji Saka came not with armies and weapons, but as a humble young man who moved in to live with a poor, elderly couple in the kingdom. When the day came that his surrogate father was selected for the king's meal, Aji Saka volunteered to be a substitute, against the protests of his adopted parents. He faced the king, and through superior wit and mystical power transformed the day of despair into victory by catapulting the cannibal king into the sea where he was turned into a crocodile. Aji Saka proclaimed liberty to the jubilant citizens of the kingdom and promised freedom and protection to all who chose to unite with him. Those who chose not to come under his protection would fall prey to the bitter, sulking crocodile giant, Dewatacengkar.

Through the Aji Saka story Tjokrosentono says to his fellow Javanese, "Long ago our ancestors walked on the Way of truth and salvation. They personally knew the only Deliverer that Almighty God provided for the redemption of all men. And they passed the knowledge on to us, but they did it in the Javanese way, very subtly. They wrapped their message thoroughly so only the wise and perceptive would recognize it. In our day, God has opened our eyes to understand and receive this message of His salvation."

The Javanese people love to use words both to disguise and to reveal — to disguise from the unlearned, and reveal to the astute. Names of people and places have meaning. The name of the wicked king means *ignorant of God*. The kingdom name, Medangkamulan, means *blanketed in the sword of oppression.* Aji Saka means *the pillar that is worthy and dependable,* like the main support pillar of a house — solid, strong, and utterly trustworthy to protect all those who live in the house.

The redemptive analogy is immediately apparent. The vicious cannibal king aptly portrays Satan seeking whom he may devour. Aji Saka's youthfulness and unselfish, even sacrificial, concern for the oppressed, combined with his unyielding grip on the forces of True Life, make him an exciting hint or shadow of the ultimate Savior.

MORE THAN JUST 20 JAVANESE CHARACTERS!

We noted earlier that King Aji Saka is the reputed creator of the Javanese alphabet. Its 20 characters originally were written in a flowing script, but now they have given way to a Romanized alphabet. All school children still study the old script, and even non-literate Javanese can chant the old alphabet. It is the written embodiment of the genuine Javanese language.

Javanese Alphabet With Equivalent Roman Characters

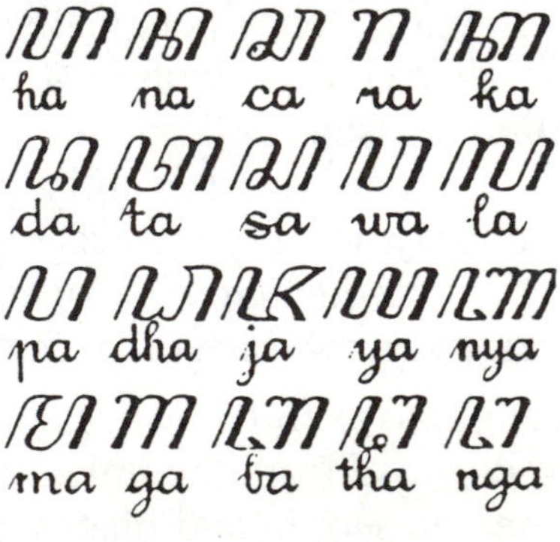

ha na ca ra ka

da ta sa wa la

pa dha ja ya nya

ma ga ba tha nga

But they are more than just 20 characters! As Tjokrosentono explains, through the alphabet Aji Saka has presented, albeit in the disguisingly revealing (or is it revealingly disguised?) Javanese style, a crucial life–and–death message for Javanese people. Presenting a message in a straightforward manner is just *not* the Javanese way — examples of that intentional, usually playful, obscurity run the range from very formal speeches at weddings to the common ways of guiding and training children.[3]

According to Tjokrosentono, the original correct order of the four lines of characters was different from the current version. Moving the third line into second place shows the message Aji Saka intended. But, remember, he was playing the Javanese game of disguising the truth so only the clever can see it. Apparently the correct order of the *Askara Jawa* — the alphabet — is:

Ha	*Na*	*Ca*	*Ra*	*Ka*
Pa	*Dha*	*Ja*	*Ya*	*Nya*
Da	*Ta*	*Sa*	*Wa*	*La*
Ma	*Ga*	*Ba*	*Tha*	*Nga*

In this order these four lines become, for the wise and informed, a statement that relates to Aji Saka's story and to the message of Salvation he left as a heritage for the Javanese people:

Hana Caraka: There was a messenger
Padha Jayanya: He was the same in power and authority as the One who sent him,
Data Sawala: He was not unwilling
Maga Bathanga: To become a dead body.

The Incarnation and Atonement in one sentence! The coded alphabet and the story of Aji Saka's deliverance of

[3]Several examples of this intentional disguising are included in the article "Aji Saka, An Eye Opener for the Javanese" *(ibid).*

the people, both mask and discreetly reveal the message of Life, that the Javanese ancestors passed down. Jesus was a messenger–redeemer equal in power and authority to the One Who sent Him. He came in humility, compassion, and power to the oppressed people of this world, and He was willing to go even to death, to set the captives free. And even now, all who come and unite with Him may escape to freedom and *slamet* far from the clutches of the Devourer.

FOOTPRINTS IN THE HILL COUNTRY

When Joyce and I saw that first footprint and began sharing it, we began looking for other "footprints" as well, that would also help open the eyes of the Javanese villagers to see their Savior, Jesus. This search for footprints motivated us to move in 1984 from the town of Boyolali to the village of Candi Baru (which means New Temple) in the high mountain pass between Mt. Merapi and Mt. Merbabu.

◊ ***Joyce*** ◊ Shortly after we moved to Candi Baru, a 35-year-old mother of three died. During the first minutes after her death and for the next seven days we were wrapped up in a drama of friends and neighbors dealing with real life. We helped in cooking, and watched as they carried water, wood and rice to serve the family's needs. Those seven days ended with a traditional feast and prayers for the soul of the mother, and also marked for us a special time of bonding into that community. Following the funeral *slametan* feast, Mickey was given a new name, *Siswa Buana* ("student from around the world") and our relationships with the people of Candi Baru were sealed in a special way.

Beyond sealing our relationships, that funeral celebration opened insights into traditional Javanese beliefs about sin and heaven.

• **Mick** • Shortly after observing the seven-day funeral feast for our neighbor, we witnessed the 1000 day remembrance for another member of that community. Gradually we pieced together the story of the "The Lamb."

The Lamb Called "The Savior"

The rural Javanese are keenly aware that God is holy *(Maha Suci)* and that He accepts into heaven only holy people. Sin is clearly a barrier to entrance to heaven. From the time of a person's death, his family is responsible to try to get rid of his sins and get the deceased's soul into heaven. At prescribed intervals of 7 days, 40, 100, 300, 600 and finally 1000 days, the relatives hold *slametans*, ritual meals, complete with the flesh of a sacrificed chicken. The community joins in pleading for the forgiveness of sins and the acceptance of the deceased into heaven.

The family's basic responsibility is discharged when they have performed the rite of *kékah* one thousand days after the death. They purchase and slaughter a young lamb with the hope and prayer that the deceased's sins are finally removed and that his soul is free to enter heaven. They believe no one can ultimately enter heaven unless he is accompanied by the soul of that sacrificial lamb who is traditionally called *Seh Juru Slamet*, meaning "The Savior." The lamb is their final hope.

A number of God–fearing traditional Javanese have been delighted to learn that Jesus is the Lamb of God, the True Savior who takes away the sins of the world (John 1:29). We have often referred to Hebrews 9:22, "...all things are cleansed with blood, and without shedding of blood there is no forgiveness," to show the close parallel between the Word of God and the Javanese practice of animal sacrifice for the cleansing of sin (both the *kékah* lamb and the more common chicken sacrifice.) We follow up with Hebrews 10:4 and 10 which asserts that "...it is impossible for the blood of bulls and goats to take away sins" because "...we have been sanctified through the offering of the body of

Jesus Christ once for all." This story of the "saving lamb," discovered during our time in the rural setting, has been a helpful "footprint" and bridge for faith.

◊ ***Joyce*** ◊ One thing that has pleasantly surprised us is the ability that God has given us to adapt to the village lifestyle. We really expected the dirt floors, limited water, little privacy, constant dust or mud depending on the season, to be difficult. but when people became the main focus — we in their homes, they in ours — the physical surroundings became less significant. Also, as our lifestyle followed more the village pattern we had more time to sit and listen to stories or to attend an all-night Javanese play put on by community actors and dancers.

• **Mick** • We found that focussing on people and choosing a life–style closer to theirs gave us a oneness with them that speaking the *words* of their language alone could not achieve. In fact, relating to people is proving to be both the best way to learn their language and at the same time the *reward* for language learning. Our evenings swapping stories and watching Javanese art forms until the final "curtain call" just before dawn, have helped in understanding another significant "footprint" or way in which God provided a hint of his promised salvation. One of these stories exists in the shadow puppet lore of Java.

The Shadow Puppet Story of Brotoseno — *In Search of the Indwelling Holy Water*

Shadow puppetry has long been a prominent form of entertainment among the rural Javanese. But its value goes far beyond entertainment. Among both the nobility and peasants the shadow puppet characters and stories are considered representative of human character and the dilemmas and struggles that men face in their life on earth. The puppeteers are considered masters of Javanese wisdom and use their influence to help shape the attitudes and lives of people by means of their clever presentation of stories and their ad libbing as a night–long performance proceeds.

A number of puppet stories may be seen as footprints leading to Christ. One story tells of a young man named Brotoseno who went in search of the key to eternal life. His pursuit brought him to the renowned teacher who revealed to Brotoseno what was needed to obtain eternal life:

> *Banyu Suci Perwitosari Kayu Gung Susuhing Angin* (The Indwelling Holy Water of Life which is the highest hope of man's heart), and
>
> *Sastro Jindro Hayu Ningrat Pangruwating Diyu* (The Highest Word which brings salvation to the world and deliverance from the *Diyu*, the Rulers of Darkness).

Brotoseno's search for the Holy Water takes him to the top of a mountain where he is stretched out between the Rulers of Darkness. The Brotoseno puppet figure appears in a crucifix-like position for many minutes, until he finally overcomes the Rulers of Darkness. He continues his search for the Holy Water of Life by obediently sub-merging himself in the midst of the sea. At this point, the puppeteer lowers the figure of Brotoseno and brings up an entirely new character. Brotoseno becomes a new creature as he has been united with the Spirit of the True God!

The Javanese have long had questions about this story, as they too have been looking for the Indwelling Holy Water of Life, and for the Highest Word. This we believe is God's provision of a "footprint" — a means by which rural Javanese can be pointed to Jesus the Son of God, the Word.

◊ ***Joyce*** ◊ The longer we stayed in Candi Baru, the more we saw our job as "dusting off" the footprints and helping our Javanese neighbors begin with what they already believed, to proceed to fuller truth in Jesus. It has also been exciting to watch Indonesians use the "footprint" concept. Pak Sastro, a Javanese co-worker, helped us find another significant "footprint." The village people intently listen to Pak Sastro's analogies between their "Secret Wisdom" *(Ilmu Ga'ib)* and the Gospel of Jesus Christ.

• **Mick** • In "Secret Wisdom" (a belief deeply ingrained in many rural Javanese regardless of their religious allegiance) there are seven basic Life Forces which are frequently abbreviated to *Four Basic Life Forces:*

Ingsun — True God
Gusti — Lord
Kawula — Servant, Radiance
Johar — Light

Many rural Javanese see life as a constant struggle against four evil spirit forces each trying to control their life. And they know that the final great struggle for mastery of their soul will come at the time of death. Will Spirit of Greed *(Aluamach*) win? Or Spirit of Fierce Anger *(Amarah)*? Or Spirit of Sexual Lusts *(Supiyah)*? Or perhaps Spirit of Judgment and Condemnation *(Mutmu'inah)*? If they conquer those four spirits, the rural Javanese hope to be united with Lord and God *(Gusti* and *Ingsun*) and then they will be allowed to experience rebirth into True Life.

The markings on the homemade blackboard took on new significance as Pak Sastro moved from the familiar teaching of *Ilmu Ga'ib* (Secret Wisdom) to:

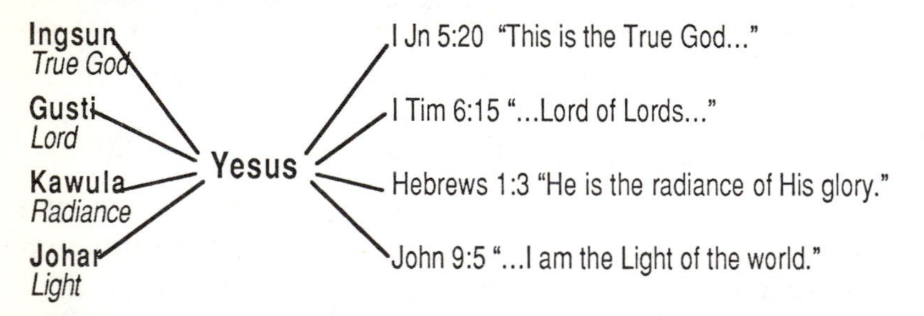

"Jesus is the fulfillment of your greatest hopes: True God, Lord of Lords, the Radiance of God's Glory, the Light of the World!"

It is no accident, insists Pak Sastro, that the 7 basic life forces are commonly reduced to 4, corresponding to the four arms of the cross radiating out from Jesus at its center!

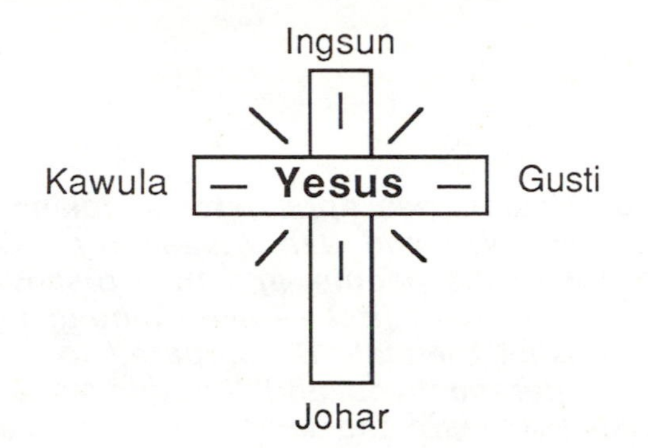

Pak Tarno (whose wife's funeral had become our bonding opportunity in Candi) seemed to come alive with expectancy when he heard Pak Sastro describe Christ as the sure fulfillment of their quest for True Life — a quest that had always been marred by "maybe" and "hopefully" under the tutelage of the Gurus of the Secret Wisdom. Pak Tarno had previously said to me, "Pak Siswo, we know of many ways to try to deal with life and death, but we are always unsure. We don't have a savior. Tell us of your Savior."

Seven months after we moved to Candi, adults from 17 of Candi Baru's 22 households joined us in a study of God's Word using as a springboard some of the "footprints" that had emerged. In May of 1985 the first believers were baptized into Christ. Others, both men and women have followed, including men from four other villages. Indonesian teachers from another church area have begun Bible lessons for the children.

The search for "footprints" has just begun. And so has the church.

◊

Sometimes missionaries appear to be taking God to the people. Ned and Nan Walker knew God was taking THEM *to the people, and they discovered He had gotten there first — even among their new Muslim friends! Be prepared to have your theological perspectives and lifestyle assumptions jarred when you learn the language, start becoming a belonger with the people and begin seeing and appreciating things from* THEIR *point of view! The Walkers experienced that, and it radically changed their approach to life and ministry.*

About ten years ago the Walkers enrolled in a language school in their chosen country but were forced to live in the community because of overcrowding in the school's living quarters. When they discovered that what they were being taught was different from what their neighbors spoke, the teachers gave them a simple solution to the problem — just don't talk with the neighbors! It was about then that they learned of a different approach to language learning. They became the first people to ask us to monitor their skill development by correspondence.

Don't Count on Schooling To Learn What Counts

by Ned Walker

"Go live in one village for five years," Bishop Stephen Neill told us. "Learn the language and get to know the people. Have your quiet time each day. At the end of five years you will be ready to serve there."

My wife and I had the privilege of asking that great missionary statesman for a friendly little tip on how to start a ministry among resistant peoples. Although this man of God sent our grand schemes of instant success plummeting, we had to admit that Bishop Neill's advice did reaffirm what we had been learning about biculturalism.

Unfortunately, said approach didn't agree with the operating policy of any mission sending agency or support constituency we had ever heard of. And our western upbringing had programmed us to do all the talking when we hit foreign soil, and to expect results instantly if not sooner. We had just finally brought to a close a long and arduous academic preparation for the mission field (which collectively included 3 years of college, 6 years of university, 5 years of seminary and earning 5 different academic degrees). The idea of "waiting" for five more years to "do something" did not seem very exciting.

As we thought about these "problems," we suddenly remembered the sly smile that framed the Bishop's lips when he was dispensing his advice. That man knew he was throwing us into a quandary, and he probably enjoyed it. He probably also knew that these very "problems" are the real reasons resistant people are resistant. Well, we must confess, out of the ton of advice we received before we soared overseas to Anobiland, Neill's words were ones that planted seeds of wisdom in us and would later bear fruit.

Our arrival as new missionaries was probably typical. We had studied about our destination and anticipated workplace. Hoping for the best, we prepared ourselves for the worst. Statistics and reports on poverty and cruel social conditions were at our fingertips and ground into our consciousness. As our plane approached our destination, we anxiously asked ourselves what it would really be like.

Peering intensely from the plane window, we could see wide green fields. That looked inviting.

But then we were there. Terrible heat. We expected that.

Some missionary friends were waving from the observation deck—a welcome sight.

The airport was undersized, crowded, and dirty. That's just what we expected.

Short–tempered customs and immigration officials were gruff and unfriendly. We had heard that the people were meek and docile.

Speaking of people — there was an ocean of them just beyond the restricted area. These were not helpless passive types, waiting with open arms for liberators from the West. They were pushing and shoving. Each one plainly had his own agenda to carry out. Dress ranging from sport coats to torn undershirts revealed the extremes of rich and poor. Completely veiled women and others with heads and waists exposed indicated a diversity of religious persuasions.

At this point we were "rescued" and guided through the mob by our friends to a nearby four–wheel–drive vehicle. This protective cocoon allowed us to observe the beggars, travelers, vendors, policemen, and others from a safe distance as we moved onto the highway toward the next intriguing destination, the missionary guest house.

Out of desire to avoid any appearance of materialism we never asked specifically what kind of housing we would have or what food we would eat. We wanted to be willing to accept anything. We were actually surprised and relieved to find electricity, running water, showers and decent beds awaiting us. Things were not stateside quality but we were not living in grass huts either.

We stayed in the large westernized capital city about two weeks and had remarkably little to do with the local people during this time. The veteran missionaries had worked hard, with the best of intentions, to conduct for our group of rookies a well–planned and busy orientation schedule — which consisted mainly of teaching sessions led by the veteran missionaries. The real highlight of this time was a meeting where we were introduced to several major national–church leaders and had a time to exchange questions and views with them. These men were at times forceful and stern, but they were evangelicals like us, so we actually enjoyed their admonitions to us to stick to the clear teachings of the Bible and avoid "church theology."

A national coup d'etat occurred on the day we were to travel from the capital to the small city where we would enroll in language school. The National palace was under siege, and few ventured out in the streets that day. But such was our determination to arrive in time for classes that we made the trip anyway. We felt that we could accomplish little until we were safely under the tutelage of professional language teachers, and under no conditions would we want to miss a day.

Normally, students of the language school lived on campus or on one of the nearby mission compounds. A record enrollment resulted in insufficient housing space. Alas, we were among the "unfortunate" couples that had to live in rented apartments in the middle of town. This simple fact was to have big implications for us, although we didn't realize it when we moved into our small three–room flat. Our neighbors were friendly and seemingly anxious to spend time with us. Diplomatically but resolutely we let them know that we were serious, full–time language students. Time for mere socializing would be very limited!

Language study at first seemed to be what we needed. The school we attended was considered the best for our new language. The instructors were native speakers who had been taught to use a "conversational approach." Things began to sour somewhat, however, when we actually were able to do some conversing. We found that the way we were learning to speak at school was different from the way our neighbors at the apartment were speaking. Our instructors very cheerfully offered a solution to this problem. They told us *not to talk* with our neighbors unless it was absolutely necessary! This situation was really the tip of an iceberg–size problem that we would spend the next several years struggling with.

The school was run by Christians — a tiny minority in the country. All of our neighbors were Muslims. It was a surprise to learn that members of these two communities spoke very different dialects of the same basic language. Muslims had borrowed hundreds of words from Arabic and Persian, which Christians refused to use because they did not want to associate with Muslims. Moreover, non-muslims claimed that their language was the unadulterated, pure one and the language school felt it was not doing its job if it didn't teach the "true" language. We were convinced that our goal should be learning how to communicate *with* the people, but we could not escape the academic effort to teach us a form of the language that most people did not use. After several months though, we found an alternative to the language school approach when we came across the *LAMP* book and discovered how to learn language in the community. Finding that the book's ideas affirmed what we had been discovering for ourselves, we began spending more time with our neighbors and less time in the house.

UNEXPECTED LESSONS!

Our problem with the language school started when we learned some quite unanticipated lessons from our neighbors. We had heard many unfavorable things at school about their culture. We were the first western people to live in that community and a few religious leaders objected to this. However, we were actually humbled by the many ways that our new friends helped us.

We had come prepared to help them, so we thought, but the roles were definitely reversed that first year. Other things about our neighbors also impressed us positively — their strong family ties, emotional security, and genuine awareness of the presence and power of God. Before I ever attempted to broach the subject of our faith, my closest neighbor mentioned to me that he prayed for me every day that I would have a safe and successful stay in his country! He was completely sincere. I was humbled.

There is no end to the stunning learning experiences we had in those days. One day I was talking to one of the young boys who lived upstairs. "Mr. Walker," he asked "Your religious leader, do you refer to him as Jesus?"

"Yes, I do," I replied, not knowing what he was thinking.

"Mr. Walker," the boy said, in his most important-sounding, but respectful voice, "I have always been taught to refer to him as *'Hojrat Isa Ruhullah Alaihisalam'* (Blessed be the Lord Jesus, Spirit of God). It is disrespectful to use less than his full title!"

I was humiliated. Could it be that this people that I had come to reach for the Gospel were going to teach me even about how to honor my Lord?

Before we went to Anobiland we did not intend to work primarily with Muslim people. We agreed with the idea that it would be wiser to work with the polytheistic groups that had shown more receptivity in the past. But the discoveries we made through our relationship with our neighbors eventually caused us to throw out that strategy. We began to realize that these people had never really had the opportunity to accept or reject the Good News. Some of them had been preached to but never communicated with.

A barrier had been erected between the Muslim people and the message of the Gospel. This has been caused by many factors — misinformation about the Scriptures by Muslims, rejection of Muslims by national Christians and offensive cultural practices by Westerners. For example, when we first began language study we purchased bicycles and rode these to school along with other couples. Our neighbors were too polite to show their shock at such behavior by women. Later we understood the inappropriateness of this. We were disappointed that no missionaries had warned us about it.

Unfortunately, Christian communication to the Muslims was through either a polytheistic or a western culture. The Christian community was formed by converts from the polytheistic community. Their Bible, of which they were very proud, used the same religious terms as their old community. This was proper for them but a disaster for the Muslims. The Christian message of a great God Who seeks to save and gather men to Himself was hidden behind a cloak of what looked like idolatry to the Muslims. As believers in one God, Muslims want to totally avoid any association with idolatry. Coming to understand these things through our language learning relationships, gave us hope and direction in beginning a ministry to Muslims.

For example, we found a lot more diversity among Muslims than we expected. Many Muslims seek a relationship with God that is more personal than what they can find by trying to obey the ritual laws. However, they do not want to be dominated by the West in this area as they have been in many others. Realizing our limitations we still began to see ways in which we could help people discover the truth and relevance of the Scriptures for their lives.

Living closely with the followers of Islam gave us a perspective we would have missed otherwise. For one thing, we were forced to face and deal with a deep–seated fear and dislike of Muslims. (Do most westerners harbor these feelings unknowingly?) The people themselves dissolved much of this prejudice by the sincerity and hospitality they showed us. Many things had struck us as absurd and irritating, including the Islamic forms of worship — reciting the Koran by memory in Arabic which they didn't understand, fasting in the day but feasting at night for one month, and bowing five times a day in a mechanical fashion. Our casual evangelical church forms crashed head–on with their idea of worship, and their strict divisions of men and women in a hierarchical social system clashed with our American ideas of equality. We believed we loved them and were sacrificing so much for them ... yet, we wondered what kind of love it was that allowed us to despise so much of their way of life. We found that what we had thought was love was only an abstract feeling we had for people we did not really know.

Through our language learning relationships our attitudes began to change. We discovered the difference between learning *about* people and learning to *know* those people, just as we had discovered the difference between learning about a language and learning to use it. Not until we really knew the people were we able to say whether or not we really loved them.

For our second year of language learning, our mission allowed us to move to another town and learn language exclusively through relationships with the local people. This was an exciting year, as a kind of "surrogate family" adopted us. Our understanding of our new country grew greatly as we watched, listened and learned.

We will never forget the learning experiences, such as the first time we took baths in the river — fully clothed like everyone else — and then had to change our wet clothes into dry ones with half the local villagers watching. This was a feat for Nan, as she was still new at wearing the local dress. People in Anobiland never disrobe and we were learning how awkward this could be to the uninitiated!

We were changing. Things that had seemed ridiculous began to make sense. Our friends needed salvation, but we began to visualize their salvation being expressed in ways unique to Anobiland. At this same time we were thrilled to hear of some Muslims who had discovered the Gospel and who were already beginning to communicate it to their kinsmen in culturally appropriate ways. Just as we had hoped, when the Gospel was removed from the filters of polytheism and western colonialism, Muslims listened and some believed.

We know one man who seriously began studying the Gospels when he observed believers from his own community thanking God for the forgiveness of their sins and the promise of eternal life. He later became a believer himself and a leader of others.

CONTEXTUALIZING THE GOOD NEWS

Not all the missionaries shared our perspective or our enthusiasm for repackaging the Gospel to accommodate Muslim thinking. Before long, it became apparent to us that a new version of the scriptures would be needed for new believers from Muslim backgrounds. Some of the missionaries and most national Christians were totally opposed to the idea. Controversies swirled around religious vocabulary. Some asked, should a believer use the word *Allah* for God?

Debates were also raging concerning retention of certain Islamic worship styles by Muslim believers. For decades most missionaries and national leaders have insisted that converted Muslims become members of their western churches and forsake all the forms of their Islamic heritage. This was done in the name of unity, while, ironically, at the same time they upheld each church's right to maintain its *own* denominational identity and independence!

For a Muslim, the price of joining one of those churches is high. He is expected to change his name, for example. All Muslims are given religious names at birth. Many are named after Biblical prophets. Nevertheless, they are expected to discard those names and adopt new "Christian" names like Dennis, Ron, Edward, or Steven. This seemed incredible to us.

A tremendous amount of time and energy went into efforts to achieve a consensus on these issues. Only moderate progress was made. In the end, the Muslim believers themselves would have to decide.

Eventually we realized that the church–missionary complex was not the best base for us to work from in reaching Muslims. So we decided to seek employment within the country. This took several years of schooling, making applications, cutting through red tape, but the benefits have made it all worthwhile. Now we are not looked on as the property of the churches the way the professional missionaries are. Thus we are free to spend all our available time with Muslims. We relate to the believers as equals, since we work in full–time employment just as they do, and like them we live with the tension of wage earning, family raising, and carrying on a viable ministry to others as God enables. In teaching Muslim believers we do not offer them the option of leaving their community to join a Christian ghetto. At the same time, however, we do not see in Scripture any reason to make life more difficult by asking them to leave all their cultural practices, as many have been expected or required to do in the past.

Lack of ministry time is supposed to be a disadvantage of the tentmaker approach. On the contrary, we have found enough time and opportunity for witnessing and teaching to allow for a balanced lifestyle that serves as an example to our believer friends who have no chance for getting support to do ministry activities full–time. In our technical field we have contact with some people that we could not have met otherwise. We avoid some of the suspicion that is often focussed on professional missionaries. Our day-to-day work and life keeps us in touch with the daily concerns of the people. We are still learning, and practical problems and insights from our work often serve to make our teaching relevant.

If someone were to come to us today for advice on how to start a ministry in another country like Anobiland, our answer may come as a shock, but our experience has shown it to be effective. First, arrange to live there for several years as university students. In addition to any formal studies, learn to speak the language by living as friends and guests of the people. Pray for guidance to one particular unreached people group and, once you find it, concentrate solely on getting to know and love them. During this same time become acquainted with all the opportunities that might be open for long–term residence. This might include mission agencies, development agencies, commercial firms, and educational institutions. Above all, pray daily that the Lord Himself would be pleased to come and live among the people through you.

◊

Randy and Edie went to live among the Turkana — a people described by outsiders as "proud, aggressive, hostile, and persistent beggars." During their language learning year, the Nelsons spent time sitting under the stars talking with their Turkana friends, and learning to understand and appreciate the Turkana people and their customs. Although at first the begging was irritating, they learned to respond to it in the Turkana way — by devising elaborate humorous tall tales to explain why they could not comply. And they even learned to "beg" appropriately themselves!

We know of no more effective way to learn the culture than by intensely living with people and learning through relationships. If one is only an outside observer of a culture, then conclusions might be drawn based on interpretations that fit the observer's outside frame of reference. To learn and experience a culture from the inside gives an opportunity to gain cultural perspectives and knowledge that might be used redemptively to bring people to Christ.

When studying language in school, language is often isolated from its normal cultural context. But child learners as well as the spontaneous adult language learners of the world demonstrate that it is more normal to learn language and culture simultaneously, through relationships. A key advantage of non-school learning is that culture learning, cross-cultural relationship skills and ministry opportunities are all gained in the same process.

I Like Your Shirt — Give it to Me!

by Randy and Edie Nelson

"What are you doing?" we were often asked during our first year among the nomadic Turkana people.

"Oh, just learning the language," we would reply with a shrug. During our early language learning time we did not feel as though we were accomplishing much at all other than providing entertainment for one small village in the form of our hilariously mispronounced words. We were just sitting around talking to people!

Like so many other eager language learners, we did provide our neighbors with plenty of opportunities to have a good laugh. For example, Edie went around for two weeks asking everyone in sight, "Is it going to rain again today?" Our location was a desolate desert that hadn't seen a drop of rain for 18 months. She thought she was asking if the rains would come soon! She would then continue, "You *must* let me go home now." No one ever refused!

We lived in an oversized mud house that was luxurious by Turkana standards. The thatched roof provided cool relief from the intense desert heat. Despite having a gas stove and kerosene fridge, "just living" took most of our time. The nearest muddy water was a mile away — a hand–dug well in a dry river bed. We wondered if, in our efforts to live close to the people, we would ever find time to learn the language. Culture shock and difficult living conditions cut our productivity in half. And we were frequently being interrupted by casual visitors from our host village. We did, in fact, try to learn the Turkana phrase, "I am busy," only to discover that no Turkana word for "busy" existed. Situated about fifteen yards from the nearest cluster of grass huts, our house became a popular visiting center for passersby. Every afternoon anywhere from three to fifteen visitors gathered on our veranda and talked animatedly as we struggled to follow the conversation.

What a surprise then, at the end of a year of irritating interruptions and of just "sitting around talking to people," to realize that we were conversing fairly well in the language of the Turkana tribe! Not only that, we appreciated the people and culture in a deeper dimension. In time, relationship–oriented language learning led us into relationship–oriented ministry. It made all the difference in the world.

We were recently talking to a young couple who had been in Kenya just a few months and were discouraged because development projects had side–tracked them from their goal of language learning. "Learn it at all costs! You may seem uncooperative to others — but learn that language!" we practically begged them. "It will make all the difference in the world."

LEARNING TO BEG!

Learning the language from the people who spoke it enabled us to like and respect the Turkana people despite aspects of their culture that grated against ours. What we had heard about these desert nomads before we arrived was barely encouraging. Yes, we had read that they were proud, independent, and hardy survivors of their harsh desert environment. Yet they were repeatedly described as hostile and aggressive, and as persistent beggars.

The Turkana custom of begging was in fact very difficult for us to deal with. The word, *nakinai* (give me) was practically an official greeting in Turkanaland. No shame or embarrassment was associated with aggressively demanding gifts, even from a total stranger. This seemed to conflict with their apparent pride and self–reliance.

We have come to feel, however, that in the traditional form, "begging" is not the right word to describe this custom. It is, for the Turkana, a good system of insurance for unexpected calamity in their survival existence. If one's animals all die and starvation threatens, it's time to call in past debts for gifts given. In real–life terms, though, the unrelenting demands for our belongings were an irritation. We simply didn't know how to cope with these demands. Living and sharing God's love with a people that we didn't like or respect was going to be difficult! Edie wrote home in the first month of language learning and described an encounter with this custom:

> This morning I went out to practice language and got into an interesting conversation with an old lady who kept calling herself *akimat* (old woman). The way she said it, it took on a whole new pitiful dimension. She touched her eyes and closed them in a realistic imitation of blindness, hung her head, let her hands fall limply by her side, and started shuffling around in a hopeless circle, mumbling *akoro* (hungry). Considering her very healthy state a moment earlier, it was worthy of an Oscar. Everyone burst out laughing, including me. Tomorrow *I'm* going to learn some phrases for begging, such as 'Give me tea, I'm dying of thirst.'

As we began to learn to joke with our new neighbors in their own dramatic way, and even to ask of *them,* the "begging" became less a problem and more an opportunity to have fun. One of the best ways to deflect unwelcome requests was to devise elaborate, tongue–in–cheek stories to explain why we couldn't give. The Turkana seemed to relish opportunities to share tall tales and laugh uproariously. Letters home trace our progress in learning to interact. At three months Edie wrote:

> I've gotten very good at turning down the constant requests for food and clothing. I'm as dramatic about it as they are! I was meekly saying, 'I only have a little food,' and my Turkana friend taught me to say, with great expression, 'I hardly have any food, just a tiny bit, and I absolutely can't give you any!' That's the Turkana way, and everyone seems to enjoy the whole process, even getting turned down.

To complicate matters, there were many desperate needs that we knew really must be met, and we often gave to those who seemed in this category. Had we not been able to respond to the constant demands in a way that communicated to the community and was acceptable to them, our frustration would have led to resentment. Resentment in turn would have engendered dislike and hampered attempts to minister God's love. Instead, we gradually came to accept the supposedly hostile ways of our neighbors.

Randy was walking from one village to the next one day and passed a thatched dome hut where one elderly man sat in the shade. Stopping to chat, Randy admired the man's beautifully carved walking stick; then, taking his cue from the Turkana, demanded, "Give me your walking stick." The old man promptly handed over the cane, and a few days later turned up at our door to ask for a cup of sugar. The exchange of gifts formed the basis for a growing friendship.

Sometimes our attempts to behave like the Turkana backfired. Once we facetiously requested a goat and were given one! The gift of the goat entwined us in a complicated system of *lopayekang*, where one is eternally indebted to his best friend. Our new *lopay* soon demanded every belonging in our house. Slowly and painfully we learned acceptable ways to extricate ourselves from our mistakes. We learned, for instance, that it was possible to say, "I don't want to be your *lopay*," and still be friendly. These discoveries went hand in hand with the daily language learning process. During that first year, having an entire village of "best friends" making daily demands at our door was nerve–wracking! But, in time, the experience of this *lopay* concept would become a tool to illustrate the gift of salvation.

Near the end of our first term when opportunities for sharing the "words of God" seemed to be exploding, Randy was able to explain to groups of men that eternal *lopay* friendship — on the highest plane — was available with God Himself. God gave the greatest gift ever given, through His son Jesus Christ, so that He could establish friendship with man. The idea of a personal God who desires friendship with man and communicates with him was revolutionary to the animistic Turkana we had come to know.

GAINING CULTURAL INSIGHTS

The insights we gained into the culture were an exciting payoff from our language learning efforts. As we spent hours with our language helper and with other Turkana people, we learned a lot about how they perceived their world. A letter home related:

> Our language helper, Daniel, has been telling us a lot of interesting things about Turkana life... How a man can track a camel for miles and tell by its hoofprints where it has gone. And how the scarred marks on some men's arms mean they have killed someone in battle. He also told us that when he was little, his

parents explained to him that God used to live on the earth but that the people pushed him back up to heaven with a big stick.

Several evenings a week we sat outside looking up at the stars and chatting with a small group of Turkana friends. They described how the moon went to sleep each morning just beyond the horizon. The stars, they said, were God's cooking fires. During these seemingly idle hours, they told about their dreams and explained that these dreams were really visitations from the spirits of the dead who lived up there somewhere in the sky. Earlier they had told us that there was no spirit world. Man was just like the animals — when his body was gone, so was he.

"Well," we asked, "where do the spirits in your dreams come from, if we all disappear when we die?"

As usual when we asked questions about spiritual life or about God, there was heated discussion and then the answer: "We just don't know. We are only human beings. Only God knows."

Some nights there was no moon at all, and the intense darkness was eerie beyond any experience of two city–bred Californians. We could have lit a kerosene lantern but it would have attracted too many poisonous nocturnal spiders. So we sat in the dark listening to the fear–filled rumors of imminent bandit raids and empathized all too well with the vulnerability of our small village. We, too, had no bright lights, no guns, no physical protection against the threat of bandits. Finally, when an attack did come one night after weeks of agonizing suspense, bullets flew through our flimsy roof and we lay flat on the floor, praying very earnestly indeed! Our Turkana neighbors, however, had no God that they knew to pray to, and no refuge from the pervasive fear that controlled their existence. Solar power now lights our more bug–proof, western–style house, but that year of living in the darkness with the Turkana people gave us an understanding of their vulnerabilities and needs. It's a joy now, to share about the freedom from fear that is available through Christ.

During those long lazy hours of talking, eagerness to get on with the work sometimes overcame us. Being language learners was alright for a while, but we had come to help the Turkana both physically and spiritually, and we were ready to get on with it. Gradually, though, the realization sunk in. Those idle hours spent sitting and talking were not a *means* to an end. That *was* our work! We wanted to share a personal God, and that was impossible without building relationships. There could be no shortcuts to language and culture learning or to effective ministry. We would need a solid foundation of appreciation and respect for the people.

One of the first things we came to respect about our new neighbors was their ability to laugh. Each night we went to sleep to the sounds of village life: raucous arguments, children crying, storytelling, lullabies, and laughter. The hearty laughter was a Turkana trademark.

"What," we often wondered, "do they have to laugh about?" They lived on scanty portions of milk and corn meal mush. Sugar for tea was a rare and exotic treat. Camel or goat meat might enhance this bland diet once a month or so. Finding forage and water for the herds was a constant challenge. Sickness and death were a part of life. One lunchtime as we sat eating cheese sandwiches and looking out our window, we saw a lumpy gunny sack being bundled out of a hut next door and carried off into the wilderness — a young mother of two had died the night before. As two young Americans, we came face to face for the first time with the reality behind those magazine pictures we had seen of a suffering world. Yet the Turkana not only survived their harsh existence, they laughed and joked and enjoyed life!

When a foreign visitor said, "The Turkana really are like children, aren't they?" we were stunned. How different our perception was! True, they didn't understand western concepts of time or money management, but shrewd wits were necessary to choose the best grazing location, evade enemy raiders and keep the herd multiplying. We were in awe of the families who headed off for a three–day trek carrying only a cooking pan, a water gourd, a walking stick and a spear.

It was more difficult for us to appreciate the way one is forced by the language to express requests in the command form. Thus, Randy couldn't say,

"Please slaughter this goat for me…"

…and Edie couldn't say, "Please help me wash clothes."

It had to be, "Come in!" "Sit down!" "Eat this." "Go away." The tones in which these commands were given sounded so peremptory, too. Not only that, to get another person's attention, a finger was often waved in the face and the request was prefaced with *"Iyonga!"* (You!).

We soon learned to talk their way; it was how we were taught by our neighbors. When we tried to soften the commands by speaking in what we felt was a more polite and gentle tone of voice, we very often were not understood. The automatic resentment we felt at first for those abrasive tones faded as we came to use them ourselves and we realized that no anger or rudeness was inherent in the words.

Another thing that was difficult for us to understand or respect was the lack of apparent gratitude in Turkana life. Many times, when we gave someone a special gift, the only response was total impassivity. No sign of gratitude at all was expressed, unless it was to request a further gift. We were not the first foreigners to feel hurt by this. One day Randy attended the one–year birthday party of a toddler, held by his parents for all the adult friends. Roasted goat meat and warm sodas were consumed by the guests, many gifts were presented, everyone laughed and had a delightful time. But not one word of thanks or appreciation was expressed by any of participants. On the way home, recalling the totally blank looks on the parents' faces, Randy somewhat tentatively asked,

"I guess they didn't like their gifts very much, did they?"

"Oh no," his friend protested. "They liked them very much. They were really happy!"

Obviously, we were missing something!

Did they have their own mysterious ways of expressing gratitude that we couldn't hear? Or was it just that one was expected to share and saying thanks was not necessary? Perhaps it was simply that in a culture untouched by Christian influence the expressing of gratitude did not exist.

The language learning process afforded us some additional insight. The word for "want" and "need" was the same. *"Asaki,"* meaning "I want" is synonymous with "I need." What a contrast to our own American culture. We thought back to a typical Christmas in our homeland, as each person anxiously wondered if each relative was receiving a gift that they really could use or would like. No wonder we need to hear "Thank you" to know that our gift is appreciated. Among the Turkana, the need was obvious. It was foolish to ask one of the perpetually thin children, "Do you want some food?" Gratitude for any gift is known and obvious, and doesn't require verbalization.

It would be wrong to imply that we blindly admired every aspect of their culture. We still have unanswered questions about some aspects of Turkana life, and many things in their culture (as also in our own) need to be influenced by God's love. To us, the pervasive indifference to the suffering and need of others was always an upsetting part of Turkana life. One Turkana pastor told us, "To love each other is what my people need to learn the most."

Although they didn't operate on principles of caring for each other, they survived through mutual interdependence. It was important for us to be dependent on them in some way as we attempted to fit into their lives as best we could.

WE NEED EACH OTHER

Our orientation in language and culture learning primed us for the learner role rather than the role of the benefactor. Thus, we were able to become friends, not just dispensers of goods and services. This turned out to be invaluable. Although we were astronomically wealthy by Turkana standards, and couldn't hide our belongings, we did depend on them in other ways. They came to us for food, but we needed them for social life. We had no other family or friends for three months at a time. We had no one else with whom to share our concerns, questions, and joys. We really did need each other and they sensed it. Another letter illustrates this:

> The pump broke down again today so we have to get our water from a hole in the river bed ... muddy but alright for laundry. Sara, my *napayekang* (best friend), helped me haul water from the local well. I carried one very small bucket and she carried a huge laundry tub full on her head. Then, she demanded payment! She seems to want traditional Turkana culture only when it comes to asking me for things. So I said, 'Okay, I'll pay you and then you won't be my *napayekang* any more.' 'No, no, no,' she hastily changed her mind and kept asking me if I was happy or unhappy. I thought I had offended her, but her parting line was, 'Tell Randy I'm coming to ask for his shirt tomorrow' — smiles, etc. When I got home, the little piece of meat I had requested from her was on the

table — a whole camel leg bone. It looked exactly like a dinosaur bone!

By our third year when opportunities developed for itinerant evangelism to remote nomadic homesteads, earlier lessons helped open doors. Randy carried little or no food on his trips out to these homes. Although he risked losing some weight, it was important that he be dependent on his hosts. He was able to sit and talk in a leisurely way rather than rushing in bent on accomplishing great things. Sometimes he managed not to grind his teeth when after a twenty–minute lesson the head elder announced "nap time" and all the men lay down on the sand for a rest. He had learned not to be completely disillusioned when his carefully prepared, heart–felt message was interrupted with, "I like your shirt. Give it to me."

There was a subtle difference when we completed our official year of language learning and moved to a different village to begin our "work." We retained our new–found abilities for making Turkana friends, and benefited from much that we had learned in our first year. However, somewhere in our minds we were not stumbling novices anymore. We knew something. Perhaps we thought we knew a lot. Interestingly, our relationships in the new working location, while friendly and warm, were never quite as deep as they were that first year. Fortunately, it was only a matter of another year or so until we felt that we knew nothing at all again!

Just as we were ready at last to plunge into our ministry, the people we wanted to reach all moved away! Inter-tribal raiding caused the herders to scatter across the desert wastes as far as 200 kilometers away. "Unreached" began to seem like "unreachable" after all.

In time, God opened a remarkable door through contact with a Christian Turkana man, formerly a prophet and diviner, who requested us to come and teach him the Bible.

Although he lived a four-hour drive away, we visited him as often as possible. Nangodia, the ex-diviner, kept referring to "about a car-load" of relatives just over the next hill who believed what he had taught them. When Randy and Nangodia at last visited the scattered homes, the "car-load" turned out to be over a hundred Turkana who asserted, "We believe in Jesus, the Son of God."

After furlough we moved again, not to a town or even a village, but to live next door to Nangodia's home in what most outsiders describe as "the middle of nowhere." In reality it is the center of a nomadic community and a fledgling church.

This exciting beginning came about through relationships — through our family's friendship with Nangodia's family over five years, and through his desire in turn to share his faith with his friends and relatives. Even today we sometimes still feel as though all we're doing is "just sitting around talking to people." At those times we remember the principle we learned during our first couple of years — our "work" *is* people.

◊

In a letter to us, Doug Curry wrote: "I have just returned to the city from my village in the hills and I am in the process of getting back in touch with the larger reality. What a privilege it has been to live in a scaled-down world with a finite horizon and a manageable number of significant relationships. To arrive empty-handed among the poorest of the poor and to be richly blessed by the warm and open welcome I received. The privilege of being adopted into the clan, to be called 'Brother,' instead of 'Sir'."

Doug has been led out of the traditional missionary role and has come to be at peace with the nonconventional posture God has called him to. We need some good models for this kind of ministry, and Doug's life offers one.

He is a bit of a romantic and a poet, and in this account Doug has captured some gems from his life in the Himalayans, that point to the One who goes before and calls all men to follow Him in life's great adventure.

Windows Into My World

By Doug Curry

"When will you come back?" my brother asked me. "We have raised the roof so you won't bump your head and have put in windows because we know you like sitting by the light."

A chapter in my life's History book was coming to a close. It was time to say goodbye. Around me sat my adopted "family," warm familiar faces, smiling through the hazy smoke and flickering fire light. We had known from the beginning that there would come a day when my research scholarship and student visa would come to an end, but those were things of the outside world that one was allowed to ignore in this remote Himalayan hideaway.

I told my family of my desire to return, but that I would first have to get another job and some kind of government approval. I knew what the authorities thought about Christian missionary activity and that a stiff jail sentence might await a new believer or one convicted of being involved in the conversion process. I had no great technical skills and I was not sure what I would be able to do that the outside world would see as being worthwhile.

"Don't let money be a problem, we will give you a third of what we have," said Jhakti, the oldest of my two adopted brothers and the village headman. "You can either continue to live in community with us or we will give you a separate piece of land and build you your own house. As for government approval, you don't have to *do* anything, we just want you to *be* with us."

I had come as a stranger from a strange land, my possessions limited to what I could carry on my back. I was dependent on their hospitality to survive — they had taken me under their wing, culturally bumbling and awkward as I was, and had cared for me and seen me through. I found their village one day when I had gotten lost and was far off the beaten track. I had been turned out in the valley below by the high-caste Hindus that lived there because I was casteless and therefore ritually impure. Maybe it was because I was feeling discouraged that I had my head down and I missed the main trail and ended up high above the valley floor and stumbled across their village. It seemed to cling to the side of the mountain almost in defiance of the harsh alpine zone it bordered on.

They too had been rejected by the valley-dwellers and had chosen to settle on the very fringe of the arable land. Their meager agricultural production was supplemented by extensive trading trips to Tibet in the summer and India in the winter. Maybe it was due to their nomadic habits that they could identify with a wanderer and a stranger, for they took me in and cared for me. I came as one who desired to learn and it was obvious to all that I was fairly clueless, so they agreed to be my tutors. Granted, I did know a thing or two, and the fact that I had learned to knit back in Canada gave me a real "in" with the men. We were soon sitting around the fire comparing stitches and swapping stories about the highest passes we had crossed and the differences between growing wheat at 10,000 feet in the Himalayas versus the prairies of Alberta. I felt as if I had come home.

Now it was time to leave. It was hard to believe that it had been just three years ago that I had crested the last ridge, gasping for breath in the 13,000 foot, thin air, to find a whole new world stretching out below me. I knew then that I was standing on the watershed that separated the moist semi-tropical hills of the south from the cool arid mountains of the north. The plains of India lay six days walk behind me, ahead the mountains jumbled on to the Tibetan plateau, five days walk to the North. However, it was only in retrospect that I realized that I also stood at another watershed, an inner one, of attitude and spirit. Over the years that followed I recrossed many times that external barrier of mountain peaks, but I have yet to return along the way that I came on this inner journey of the soul.

Just a few months before going out to live in the village, I had written back to my prayer partners that I felt like oil on water, floating on the surface. I wrote:

> I use the term 'float' instead of 'move,' as it is a more accurate description of how I feel. In the West one 'moves'; in the East one 'floats.' At the mercy of government policy, somewhat unsure of just where you are going or the best way to get there, you 'float.'
>
> In my initial two and a half years in this country I worked with the officially recognized mission — an effective and efficiently-run organization that has encapsulated enough of the West and its momentum to allow its people to 'move.' There are certain things that one loses when one steps out of that capsule. I am beginning to understand what they are — and what the Lord and I have gotten ourselves into.

In my first term overseas when I had worked with this well-known and respected mission I was given considerable responsibility and authority. People listened to me when I spoke and I was respected and obeyed. If I had business in a government office I would be given first-class treatment, a cup of tea, and moved to the head of the line.

But for my second term I returned as a student, enrolled in a local university and became a nobody. Now that I was a student and had no organizational connections, I would be asked to wait at offices, sometimes for days. In many ways I was more frustrated and felt that I was accomplishing less than when I had been a "company man." Yet I found that the quality of relationships that I began to develop was on an entirely different plane. Now I was usually on the receiving end, dependent and in need of care. I began to understand why the Lord sent his disciples out on their first missionary outing, empty handed and dependent on the hospitality of those they were to minister to.

When I first arrived in my "chosen land," I was a recent graduate from university, I thought that I was through with school and I was ready to start doing something. Now almost ten years later when I fill out forms that ask my occupation I still put down "student." (They look at you strangely if you put "learner.")

I had learned to speak the national language during my first term, but I had never learned to communicate effectively. I had learned enough to say what I wanted, but not enough to hear what others were saying back. I could give orders, but I could not sing a love song. I had plenty of employees, but few friends. The high brick wall of the old-style compound had been replaced with an invisible barrier of misunderstanding and awkwardness that had begun to produce a fortress mentality. I knew that if I were going to do more than just survive in this "chosen land" I would have to start at the beginning and work my way up. I thought that a brief sabbatical from the institutional work of the mission would give me the opportunity that I would need to get past the goo-goo-gaa-gaa stage of cultural competence. Then I could return to take up the weightier responsibilities appropriate for one of my background and training.

When I stood at the top of the pass looking down at the jumble of ridges and valleys below I was thinking of six months to a year. But I was to learn as I went along that when one responds to the call, "Follow me," it is with no guarantee of return to the point of disembarkation. In fact the very nature of the journey precludes returning home. For the freedom of the road that allows one to become all things to all men, means that one's identity is not related to where one is from, but rather, where one is going.

What follows are some *windows into my world,* a few good old "remember when" stories that are best told sitting around a fire with a cup of something warm in one's hand.

THE OLD, OLD STORY — AT THE TOP OF THE WORLD

We were heading north toward Tibet to trade grain and cooking oil for salt and wool. Only a few minutes before, the sun had forced its way into the narrow gorge, signaling a much welcomed break. The wood had been gathered and I sat resting, a sun-warmed rock at my back, and cooking fire at my feet. The barley flour and water were mixed and the first of the flat bread was roasting on the old piece of tin — breakfast was on the way. Around me, scattered among the loads they had been carrying, sat twenty sturdy mountain men, my traveling companions these last five days. Billowing turbans framing faces weathered by sun and sorrow, creased by smiles. Calloused hands, first tirelessly spinning, then deftly knitting. A moment, frozen picture-like; bordered by canyon walls, explosions of warm fall colors mixed with cold blues of mountain streams, a soaring backdrop of icy peaks and blue-black skies.

The headman of our village, with whom I live, was leading the party and he is a firm believer that one understands by doing. I had come to learn and they have been patient with me, but I had also come to share. That morning I had read Colossians: "So, naturally, we proclaim Christ. We warn everyone we meet, and teach everyone we can, all that we know about Him ..." I had just begun to reflect on the present implications of that statement when one of the men asked what I was reading and why I read the same book every morning. And so the old, old story of

Jesus and his love was told once again and tiny seeds were scattered in the hearts of a few more of God's people.

YOU ARE WORTH MORE THAN MANY SPARROWS

It was only a young bird, hardly a week old, yet it was already dying. With string tied around a clipped wing, the little children were dragging it through the gutters outside my window. They laughed at its crippled attempts to escape and defend itself. Were they too young to understand? Who was I, a stranger and outsider to interfere? Besides it was the first time in a long while that I had heard some of these kids laugh. For the plight of the sparrow was mirrored in their swollen bellies and skinny limbs, some of them were already dying. Maybe only half would make it to their fifth birthday. The weight of injustice and suffering can be almost overwhelming in its vastness and complexity. "Where does one start?" The answer came, "Here." For I couldn't just sit and watch. Someone had to tell these little kids and their silently watching parents that there was a way out of the circle of suffering.

I tried to explain how the same God that loves both sparrows and little children, cries to see any of his creation dragged through the gutters of an unjust and unholy world. Lacking two farthings, I traded a few sweets for the sparrow, ignoring the taunts that it would never fly again and was doomed to die. Yet, sensing that the quality of life one lives is more important than how or when one dies, I chose to trust my little charge to God's mercy rather than to man's perversity. That evening I found myself high on the ridge behind the village whispering an incoherent prayer to the God of sparrows and of men. Then, with little faith, I opened my hand, half expecting a pitiful, fluttering, earthbound flight. But it flew, wobbling, half gliding, but definitely airborne. As I watched the sun set and the darkness grow it was almost like a sun was rising inside me, and there was warmth that overcame the numbness of human despair. There is hope because there is Jesus. "God had chosen what the world calls foolish to shame the wise; he had chosen things of little strength and small repute..."

IN THE PITS

JOURNAL ENTRY — 09/04/82: Good Friday was spent, at least four or five hours worth, digging the family latrine. In one corner was an old latrine, supposedly three years old, it should have been well composted. Well it wasn't! I ended up digging out the 'goo,' as the hired hand wouldn't touch it with a ten-foot pole. I kept telling myself, "An act of love, an act of love." Considering what Jesus did for me on the same day a couple of thousand years ago, it seemed like a small token of gratitude.

My Research Journal was public property and had to be turned into the university so I had to be careful what I wrote in it. The expanded story goes like this:

Hygienic conditions in the village were the pits. Or should I say that for the lack of any pits the paths between the houses were open sewers! In theory, one was supposed to use the fields on the outskirts of the village, but in the middle of the night when it's cold or rainy outside who listens to theory? I had built my own little latrine upon my arrival and had volunteered to help the family build their own when they were ready. The spring building season extends over most of April, and it just so happened that the day that Gorak decided it was time to build the family latrine was Good Friday.

I had been trying to think of something that would communicate to the people the significance of the Easter festival, but had not come up with any good ideas. I had planned to fast on Friday and Saturday and then have a sunrise service for myself on top of the ridge Sunday morning. I thought that it would be a personal affair between my Lord and me — until Gorak had decided it was time to start building our family latrine.

Level ground was at a premium and so we ended up digging at the same site that had been unsuccessfully used as a latrine in the past. It had been too shallow and had smelled and so it had been discontinued. However, I was assured that it had been many years ago, and my development manual said that three years was sufficient to see the composting process return things to their natural state. We had dug down about three feet when we hit the so-called composted section. Well, I guess the book had not taken into account the fact that we were half-way up a mountain and for the better part of the year things were in semi-hibernation. All we knew was that the smell coming up from our newly excavated pit was less than pristine and all we had were short-handled shovels! Suddenly the hired man remembered that he had a fence that needed mending, and he disappeared over the horizon. Gorak, my older brother, looked me in the eye and said, "Why don't we just forget the whole thing and just fill it back in? I am a respected elder in this village and it just wouldn't do for me to be seen down in that pit shoveling that stuff."

Well, it had taken us two years to decide to build the latrine and we were already a good way down. I knew that if we stopped now, we would never build another and, besides, hadn't I been told that a basic requirement for a missionary was a poor sense of smell and a good sense of humor? I told Gorak that I would dig out the smelly stuff and haul it away and give him a call when it was all over. So there I was, between gulps of fresh air, down in the pit cleaning up someone else's mess and trying to figure how it all fit in with Good Friday and Easter. And it did fit.

Granted I might have chosen a less graphic symbolization of what Christ did for me, but it did fit!

I was nearly to the end of the smelly stuff when Gorak reappeared on the scene, and squatted down beside the pit with a somewhat bemused look on his face. He told me he had gone after the hired hand and offered to pay whatever he would have asked if he would come back to dig the stuff out. But he would do it for neither love nor money. "Why are you doing this for us?" he asked me. So I told him what I had been thinking, how when his son messed his pants he would clean it up, out of love. I too wanted to do something "out of love" for them because they had done so much for me, but more so because of what God had done for me and what I knew He wanted to do for them. I told them how the Son of God had come to earth out of love and how He had died, giving His life to lift man out of the pit of sin and death. He had taken on our stinking sin and carried it away.

As I shoveled and talked, Gorak climbed back down into the pit and helped finish up. We were talking about the Easter story and concentrating on not getting any of "it" on us, and so at first we did not notice the crowd that was gathering. Word had gotten out that the headman was down in the pit shoveling "you-know-what," and everyone had come to see. It was like a mini amphitheater and we soon had a sizeable audience. As I told Gorak about the death and resurrection of Jesus, he passed the story on to the men around. Then he said, "We have a story like that:

> Long ago a shepherd from the hills went down to the plains of India and was walking along beside the railway tracks. He came to a bridge that had just burned out and he knew that the passenger train that was soon to come along would be derailed and many would die. He knew that the engineer would pay no attention to a poor peasant trying to wave the train down. So he went up the tracks and laid himself down

on them. When the train came, it tried to stop when they saw him, but it was too late and he was crushed to death. They did stop in time to see the burned-out bridge and understood why he had laid down his life. That is kind of what your Jesus did, wasn't it?"

The whole village heard that day of the love of Jesus and saw in a small way that love acted out in a form that they could understand. I was able to look Gorak in the eye and know that we had touched hearts and that we understood each other better than when the day had begun. Truth had been lived and spoken.

BELOVED LAMB?

The blue-black sky silhouetted the old man standing high above the crowd. Gently he held the young goat, or "Beloved Lamb" as the people called it. Below, the mass milled around a group of men swaying in unison, hands outstretched, chanting their mournful song, eyes fixed on the old man with the kid now held high above his head.

It was to be the last sacrifice of the day, but it was different than the hundreds that had preceded it. For all the previous blood spilt had been man's offerings to the gods. This was the god's gift to the people. And, as its origin was different, so would be its ending. The anticipation of the crowd began to peak as the singers' voices rose to a crescendo, pleading that the lamb be given. Then with a final plaintive bleat the young animal was thrown into the air, falling to disappear in a sea of clutching, tearing hands.

Desperately, each man vied for the privilege of being the one to disembowel the young goat, using only his teeth. Disappointed men came up with mouthfuls of hair, until finally, bloody-faced, entrails hanging from his mouth, the victor emerged to the cheers of the crowd. Could this beloved lamb of the gods point to the Beloved Lamb of God? Redemptive analogy or spiritual counterfeit?

Much has been written about redemptive analogies and they are often seen as the key that has unlocked the door that has lead to the conversion of whole groups of people. How exciting it is to think that there awaits in every culture a bridge that one can use to cross over the gap that so often separates "us" from "them." When I first saw this ritual being performed it seemed such a natural leader into the salvation story. Yet I have hesitated to take advantage of it. Partially because I am not yet sure just what significance it has to the people, and partially because I believe that in the final analysis, *I* am the dynamic equivalent.

Unless the people can see in my life the commitment and love that says that I believe in them and I'm prepared to go to the end with them, then all my cultural insights are like water off a duck's back. It comes back to relationships being the key; all the rest just greases the lock. There are no short cuts, no techniques that guarantee success. One goes because one is called. One obeys because one believes.

What I have discovered for myself is what many who have gone before have also found to be true. That is: if God calls, He will enable. A sense of inadequacy can be a blessing when combined with a clear vision of the task we have been called to. We have been commanded to believe God for great things, to take chances, to step outside the walls and face into the wind. It is not necessary to know one's destination in order to begin the journey.

May our generation be known as the age of the adventurers, those who were prepared to leave the comfort of the boat and step out on the waves in order to draw nigh unto our Lord. It is only in following Him that we discover who we are and who we are meant to be. Then we are able to share in that discovery with our fellow travelers.

◊

Endurance

By Jeanette Chaffee

Lord, remember the “biggies”?
Fears of cockroaches, snakes and heat?
How could I endure?
Yet I knew
when I left the States
that I had no choice.
It was either "take what comes my way"
or be disobedient to You.
Yes, I’ve killed a few cockroaches
and yes, I’m constantly dripping with perspiration
during the hot season. But I’ve lived through it.
And never once have I yet seen a *live* snake.

The Lord replied:
Yes I remember.
My power really does work best
through weakness.
My strength can carry you
through any situation.

The McGirrs have found that a non-school philosophy of language learning can rub off into lots of other areas of life. Randy writes, "I found myself learning not only German, but also a host of other disciplines: organization, self-motivation, creativity, problem solving, independent thinking, and personal responsibility. As the years went by we began to discover many areas of learning that we could and should take over ourselves."

As a family they have learned to be comfortable with being somewhat unconventional. One tape we received from them about ten years ago told of their temporary decision to cease using English in their home until they had learned German. They were at peace about the fact that their children would lose English for a while. For, as Randy said, "They will have the advantage of having native speakers as parents when they start learning English again."

Randy and Diane participated in one of the earliest language and culture learning courses that we taught. It was back in 1974, in Vienna. At that time only part of the LAMP *book was available, in manuscript form (in fact, it was going by the unmanageable title of "Language Acquisition Through Manageable Procedures"). We have all learned a lot since those days, and feedback from people like the McGirrs has been a big help along the way.*

Our Viennese Waltz

By Randy McGirr

We carried four suitcases and had a German vocabulary of exactly two words — *Sauerkraut* and *Gesundheit*. Anyone with a sharp eye who had seen us then would probably have thought to himself, "If they don't find a McDonalds soon, they may not survive!" It was July of 1974 and my wife Diane and I and our two small children, Randy (4) and Kirsten (1) had just stepped off the train in Vienna, Austria.

Who are we and what were we doing ten years ago in the capital of Austria?

I guess I could best describe myself back then as a rather average young father from the great plains of the Dakotas with a Political Science degree in one pocket, a Theology degree in the other, and the desire to be of some use for the Lord in Austria. Both degrees turned out to be of little help, but the desire to be of use to the Lord was the motivation that often sustained us through more than a decade of life in this little country in the Alps.

Those children are now fifteen and twelve. Both are in high school in lower Austria. A third child, Koleran, joined them nine years ago in Vienna. He is a fourth grader, plays on a soccer team, and speaks Viennese German, as we all do. We have many close friends in Austria, and we would miss them very much if we ever had to leave. We hope we won't have to!

When I look back on these ten years, my mind automatically focuses in on the many barriers we had to break through before we could truly say, "We feel at home."

How could I forget the time when I walked into a vegetable store and picked up a handful of tomatoes? A wizened old *Verkäuferin* grabbed my wrist and hit me with an avalanche of words, which I was glad I couldn't understand. I learned very quickly that you wait to be served in such a store! Pointing is allowed, but no touching! It took me a while to mend my trampled pride after that, but such incidents helped me become sensitive to the literally hundreds of ways in which Austrians see things differently from Americans. In fact, they may view almost everything differently, from the correct use of a toothpick to the deeper perspectives surrounding politics, education, religion, and family life.

It was our goal to communicate effectively in this new culture, and at the very outset we found ourselves confronted with problems which caused us to draw deeply on our ingenuity and resources.

Our first task was to find a place to live. We felt immediate pressure from American friends to live in a district where most of Vienna's 10,000 Americans live. Both an American and an English school were located in this area. We had to consciously resist this pressure. We had come to live with the Austrians. We eventually found an apartment on the opposite side of the city, which cost considerably less than a similar flat in the "American sector."

What about a car? We decided to go without, and use the public transportation. This decision proved to be an advantage in many ways and removed a big temptation from our lives. Americans are usually addicted to "driving around" and we were no exception. This addiction tends to intensify for Americans living in Europe. We found out that we didn't need a car to see the spiritual and linguistic "countryside" in Austria.

LEARNING TO TALK

We immediately began to learn German — not by attending classes in a language school, but through relationships and a process of self-directed learning. The first edition of *LAMP* proved to be a good introduction to self-directed language learning. We tracked down some university students to be our helpers, and we began putting German texts together.

We had some uphill battles before our self-directed learning really began to pay off. First, we had to struggle with the validity of the whole concept. We were accustomed to the classroom method of language learning, and we were unsure of any other approach.

In addition, we had to struggle with the development of discipline and creativity. In a school, I know when I have to be in the classroom and I know I will be assigned homework. But a self-directed learner has to take over the roles traditionally played by school and teacher. I found myself learning not only German, but also a host of other disciplines: organization, independent thinking, creativity, problem solving, self-motivation, and personal responsibility. Personal development in these areas actually turned out to be one of the major benefits of the whole self-directed learning process.

We planned our own curriculum, organized our own materials, developed exercises, collected resources, tracked down tapes, and put together a growing "army" of Austrians to be our helpers and friends. This process kept us working in German and among German speakers.

Our "school" was our home, and wherever else we happened to be.

BREAKING THE TIES

We were convinced that it would be necessary for us to leave much of our own culture behind if we were serious about "being Austrian to the Austrians." The example of Christ, who emptied himself and became a man (Phil. 2), and of Paul, who was all things to all men (I Cor. 9), reminded us that we could not necessarily hold on to our own cultural forms and values and hope to communicate the message of Christ to Austrians.

One practical application of this principle was our decision to spend as little time as possible among English speakers. It helped to not be living in the American community in Vienna. But that did not solve all the problems.

I remember once when the phone rang. It was early evening. I could hear my wife's voice, "Oh, hello Pat. Yes, we're fine. Oh, thank you, that's sweet of you to invite us ... but I'm afraid it just won't work out at that time.... Yes, I know it's been a long time. Really, I'm very sorry. Thanks for calling."

Diane turned to me and said, "I don't think people are too happy with us. They think we're antisocial."

This was a tough pill for her to swallow. She had never been antisocial in her life. But here she was, turning down an invitation to a birthday party. Why did she do it?

We had decided to hold our social engagements with English speakers to a bare minimum. We knew that we needed to immerse ourselves in our new culture and avoid those situations in which we would be thrust back into the need to speak English. Little remarks from American friends sometimes revealed that not everyone was in agreement with our strategy: "You never visit us!" or "Aren't you afraid of depriving your children?" or "You're missing so many opportunities, things you could accomplish using English right now."

This was a problem that persisted for a number of years. Most people are to some degree dependent upon close friends, people who really understand them. We were no exceptions. But the move to Austria cut us off from a number of such friends, and our decision to hold our relationships with English speakers to a minimum, pretty much (though not totally) severed any remaining bridges. Our thinking, of course, was to see such deeper relationships develop with Austrians, but this would take time. Austrians are a very conservative people, about the opposite of what we would call outgoing.

On the average, Austrians do not have a lot of friends. Often relationships are kept at a formal level which is reflected in their slow and proper way of meeting and entertaining people.

In our first year in Austria we were a bit taken aback at the difficulties we were having in establishing relationships. We were doing everything we could to come into contact with people, but progress was slow. We talked to students at the University, tried to be friendly to our neighbors, invited people to dinner, threw a few parties, and kept progressing in our language learning.

Then it happened that an Austrian college student began to take us under his wing. He would call and drop by without being invited. I'll never forget the day he gave us an old bicycle that he had bought and repaired himself. We were friends!

Through him we met many more Austrian young people. He would bring them by and invariably our discussions would turn to Jesus Christ and to matters of life and faith.

We have worked together with this young man for nine years now, and he is one of the most dynamic Christians we know in Austria. He is married, has two children, and is presently in the process of establishing a home for neglected children and for the handicapped.

THE LONG HAUL

Many things in life seem to demand a learning time of two to four years. Two years of junior high pave the way for four years in high school, which in turn lays the foundation for four years of college, which leads to three or four years of graduate school.

How long does it take to adapt to a foreign culture? It was natural for us to think in terms of from two to four years. All we had to do was put in our time and wait for graduation day. Did it work out that way?

To be truthful, we would have to say that after ten years, we are still waiting for graduation day! We have not come close to learning everything we could. Every culture is a mixture of dozens or even hundreds of sub-cultures, and every language is a collection barrel of dozens or hundreds of sub-languages. It is interesting to hear folks from Vorarlberg and Burgenland (two states in Austria) talk to one another — they both speak German, but often they can't understand each other.

After four years we finally knew enough of our new culture to comprehend how little we really knew! That was frustrating, but it was also a lesson we much needed. Cultural adaptation, particularly as it relates to communicating with people, does not necessarily consist of a "course of studies" that can be completed at some point in time. It is a dynamic process in need of constant expansion. It has helped us to accept this and to know that we will never be receiving a diploma in Austrian culture.

It was approximately at the six–year point that I began to experience some new struggles which I had not fully anticipated. The best way to describe the situation is simply to say: We had all become different. Our kids were no longer eighty percent American and twenty percent Austrian. They were now 49 percent American and 51 percent Austrian. We were well underway to becoming part of the Austrian woodwork.

Did I want that? Was it necessary? Were we making a mistake? For several months it was a struggle. I often thought to myself, "The kids are getting older and just think, my boys will never play baseball, football or golf." That's a ridiculous thought, of course, but that's the kind of thing that kept shooting through my head.

For months I remember waking up every day with a heavy feeling in my stomach. What was it? Culture shock? Selfishness? Sensitivity? Lack of faith? Fear? Loss of identity? It was probably some of all of these, combined into a genuine case of "cultural growing pains."

I weathered the storm by constantly reviewing basic scriptural perspectives and by regularly checking my priorities.

For example, I remember a time when I was very critical toward the Austrian school system. I disliked some of the experiences my children were being exposed to. I felt sorry for them. I was not under the illusion that American schools were perfect, but at least they were familiar to me. I began to wonder if my children should change schools. But as I compared the curriculums of Austrian and American schools, I noticed that there were really only differences of emphasis. The major things I wanted my children to learn were not to be found in *either* system: namely love, forgiveness, gentleness, truthfulness, goodness, joy, patience, longsuffering, etc. I could expect no school system in the world to impart these things to my children. It was my responsibility, and mine alone.

This perspective helped me to get my eyes off the externals (academics, sports, social activities, etc.) and to focus on the central issues of life.

We are now happy that we kept our children in Austrian schools. In addition to the fact that our children have had a significant outreach to their classmates, we have discovered certain things about the Austrian educational system which we very much appreciate, aspects which we were not aware of in our initial years in Austria.

SELF-DIRECTED LEARNING HELPS ESTABLISH RELATIONSHIPS

In Austria we had to learn not only a new language but also new channels of communicating and new ways of relating to people. After we had been in Austria for several years, we moved to a small village outside of Vienna. For several months we found it very difficult to meet Austrian people. They seemed suspicious and standoffish.

I used to go to the soccer field to play soccer with my sons, and this led us to one of our first acquaintances in our new town. We often saw another father there with his son and we began playing together. He then invited me to come play soccer with a group of men in the village who played every Wednesday. I was pleased to have received such an invitation and showed up the next Wednesday. My new acquaintance was the only one to welcome me and he simply said I should play on his team. For the next two hours I was ignored for the most part, and after the game no one came to me to introduce themselves or to shake my hand. That was difficult to swallow and my tendency was to take it personally. I figured, however, that there was something that I was not understanding and I kept my eyes open.

A few months later, Diane began visiting with a woman she had met while shopping. This middle–aged mother of three had not grown up in our village. She came from another state in Austria and had married into the area. She related to us that she had found it very difficult to establish any friendships with the villagers. That surprised me because she was a lovely, outgoing person. At any rate, we learned then that our contact difficulties did not simply stem from the fact that we were Americans. Here was an Austrian woman who was having problems establishing friendships even in her own country! What were we going to do? We decided to keep on learning and to keep on experimenting. This decision helped us to discover more effective ways of making meaningful contacts with Austrians.

One of these doors into the culture turned out to be *children*..

I used to ride back and forth to Vienna in the train. It so happened that I often sat next to Robert, a teenager from our village who was attending a school in Vienna. I began helping him with his homework and after a few months we became good friends. He also expressed a growing interest in Jesus Christ. It was not long before he became a regular guest in our home.

We often wondered what his parents thought of this new relationship. His father was an alderman in the town and his mother was the owner of the drug store. We often saw them, but they seemed to ignore us like everyone else. One day, when I was in the drug store, Robert's mother came to me and said, "Herr McGirr, could I speak to you in the back room for a moment?" I thought: "Oh oh, here it comes!"

Was she angry or worried? Not at all! In fact, she told me how thankful she was that I had taken an interest in Robert. She reported that he was interested in school for the first time in his life and that he had become more serious and responsible at home. They invited our whole family to dinner a week later and that was the beginning of a beautiful relationship between our two families. Within only two years Robert became one of our most effective disciples and his mother and father two of our most faithful friends and supporters.

Our house is often full of young people on the weekends, and Robert's mother and father often volunteer to furnish the whole crew with cakes, or homemade bread, or even whole meals.

As a result of this and similar experiences, I began to make it a point to cultivate relationships with young people. This channel of communication has led us right into the heart of many Austrian homes, homes which are usually open only to the nearest of friends and relatives.

In our decision to be involved more with children and teens we were faced with various challenges. How would we begin and in what capacity? After much observing and thinking I decided to start coaching a soccer team for boys the same age as my oldest son. This decision was a direct product of the new perspectives I had developed because of self-directed learning. I had never coached a soccer team before. In fact, I had never played on a soccer team, but I was convinced that I could learn quickly by collecting information, finding an assistant who was a good player, and by simply getting started. It worked.

I started out with the only boys team in town, a ragtag bunch that had never had a coach longer than two months. Three years later our village had *three* boys teams representing more than 50 players and five fathers who were coaching them. And I was right in the middle of the whole operation!

This success did not result in all the communication barriers being broken down, but we did see bridges of trust erected in the community and many doors opened to us.

A few years later, Diane decided to start coaching a girls basketball team. At the present time, between us we are coaching four teams and rubbing shoulders with 60 young people a week.

An outgrowth of this has been a camping ministry which has grown from 20 participants to more than a hundred in two years.

SELF-DIRECTED LEARNING LEADS TO FLEXIBILITY

Through self-directed learning we were constantly confronted with the need to drop ineffective methods and to be constantly on the lookout for better ways of doing things. At first this process was threatening, but as we began to see the benefits of this commitment, it actually became an enjoyable and dynamic part of our thinking.

During our first years in Austria we spent a lot of time with college students. We began meeting together regularly with those who were serious about following Christ and who wanted to learn the Scriptures. Each year, it seems, we have in some way changed our framework of meeting and working together.

Our thinking as we evaluate is: What are our goals for our family and our disciples, and how can we adapt ourselves to their situation to best reach these goals? Our reference point eventually ceased to be a "certain way of doing things" and became a dynamic process of determining goals, collecting information, reviewing, evaluating, mapping out new strategies and developing more effective methods. These are all elements of self-directed learning and we have found them to be applicable in the whole discipleship process.

SELF-DIRECTED LEARNING — GOOD FOR THE FAMILY!

Fifteen years ago we took our first wobbly steps into the world of self-directed learning — we sold our TV! We have never regretted this decision, and we never bought another one. Back then it seemed an almost radical thing to do and we were a bit apprehensive, but we quickly discovered that we didn't need to be entertained.

As the years went by we began to discover that there were many areas of learning that we could and should take over ourselves. Language learning was just one of them. We found ourselves moving further and further away from the "go somewhere to be trained" mentality, and began expecting more and more of ourselves.

We have been pleased to see the effect all of this has had on our children. Many people have commented on their wide variety of interests and on their high degree of self-motivation. Anyone who comes to our house is often struck by the whole set–up — it gives the impression of being a learning center.

We make up our own games, we read books together, and we are all learning modern Greek as an introduction to koiné Greek. Each of our children does personal study in the Scriptures, without ever having been told to. Our oldest son taught himself to play the guitar last year and now leads our song sessions. His younger brother also started guitar on his own a few months ago.

We all write lots of letters. Kirsten (12 years old), regularly sends letters to India, Italy, America, and to friends in Austria. She has also taught herself gymnastics and it is not an unusual sight to see her walking through the house on her hands!

At other times you can see us working in our makeshift film studio, drilling each other in any of five different languages, or rummaging through one of the world's most unique filing systems — we invented it ourselves eight years ago. We could also show you some interesting books that we have printed and bound ourselves.

All in all, we have come to view learning in a much broader sense. It is not an activity reserved for the classroom, but in a very real sense it is the substance of life itself. In the Scriptures, learning is connected to the whole idea of spiritual growth. To know God is the purpose of life and to learn to understand and to do His will is the process of growing into Him.

In Luke 2:52 we read that Jesus grew in wisdom (σοφοσ — understanding) and in stature (ιλικια — physical and experiential maturity) and in grace before God (spiritually) and before men (socially and culturally).

Our family has self-directed learning goals in each of these areas.

◊

Paul Bunyan Learns to Speak Rainstorm

Paul Bunyan needed to learn to talk like a rainstorm so he could coax a baby rainstorm out of a cave. Here's his plan: "I'll git me a disguise that looks like a rainstorm, then I'll go out and live with a tribe of 'em and learn their language. Should be simple enough, shouldn't it?"

And that's just what he did. He fell in with a big tribe of them, and his disguise was so perfect that they just figured he was a strange rainstorm, and they invited him to stay with them as long as he liked.

Anyway, late in the summer he came back, and just to show off he was always throwing rainstorm words into his talk, till the lumberjacks scarcely knew what he was talking about. Then one day he went over to the mouth of the cave where the rainstorm was. Getting down on his hands and knees, he put his face up close to the entrance to the cave and imitated the cry a mother rainstorm makes when she is calling her young ones.

"See thet," says Paul, with a big grin. And then he hollered the 'rainstorm holler' again, and that little rainstorm came tearing out of the cave as if he'd been sent for. He jumped into Ol' Paul's arms and licked his face like an excited puppy dog.

Ol' Paul petted him and talked to him soothingly, till he quieted down, then sent him off down to Iowa where the rest of the rainstorms are.[1]

◊

[1]From: "Baby Rainstorm," by Glen Rounds, in *Time to Laugh*, Alfred A. Knopf Inc, NY, 1942.

Joe Rouse originally went to Sierra Leone as a volunteer (under the Mennonite Central Committee's "Teachers Abroad Program"), where he lived and worked as a teacher among the Mende people for six years. He then returned to the States where he became part of a Christian fellowship and received some missionary training. Now, back in Sierra Leone, he has also been learning the Themne and Krio languages. As he puts it, "Day by day this Themne mountain is being moved."

Joe is single and maintains a simple lifestyle, living in the villages in the homes of the people. His partner in ministry, Edward Mansaray, is a Mende.

A couple years ago Joe wrote to us: "I'm a survivor after living exclusively with Africans, eating African foods with Africans in the African way, drinking unboiled, unfiltered water right from the swamps from common cups. I've been bitten by thousands of mosquitoes (and have swallowed numerous other insects), slept in local beds, and bathed in swamps and rivers. I've ridden in very tiny, tippy canoes in leach–infested waters. I've willingly eaten meat from large rats, termites, snails and monkey. And I spent an entire month in a very remote village, becoming a 'child' in Themne land."

In his article, Joe chats with us about his experiences and about the importance of deciding to overcome any obstacles that might stand in the way of learning the language.

Growing Ears for the Language

or

What if They Giggle?

By Joseph Rouse

We were already very crowded in the back of a covered pick-up truck when we stopped to take on even more passengers. The last to get in was a woman with a couple of baskets, a vacuum bottle, and a little girl about four years old. As she struggled to get in she handed the bottle to me. We finally found room for all of them and managed to squeeze the baskets somewhere under our tangle of feet, but I remained holding the bottle.

As the journey continued — hot, dusty, sweaty, bumpy — I grew tired of holding *her* bottle. Partly I was afraid I might break it. But, more honestly, I was simply put out. "Why should *I* have to be bothered to hold *her* bottle?" Finally I handed it back to her. She immediately gave it to another passenger who held it for the rest of our journey.

One young man, seeing that the little girl was not comfortable sitting on top of a sack of groundnuts, picked her up and cradled her in his lap. It was not long afterward that she began to look sick — then she *was* sick. To my amazement, this young man quickly removed his stocking cap and used it as an "emergency bag." And the little girl was sick several times. The young man treated her as if she were his own beloved daughter, speaking softly to her and encouraging her until he reached his destination and got down from the truck.

No other passenger on that truck seemed to take any notice of what that young man did for the child: he was simply doing what anyone else might have done. "Yes," I thought, "Anyone else but me! If I had been holding her, I would have given her back to her mother the moment she began to *look* sick!" I felt ashamed of my own impatience with the woman's bottle. I resolved to do better next time.

So often, in very ordinary settings like this I have learned from the people of Sierra Leone the depth of my poverty in interpersonal relationships. But, little by little, day by day, as I live with these people I am learning how to really be a neighbor and a friend. True, there are many cultural differences in the way people express caring, but what I am learning is changing my heart. I will never be the same since I've come to know these people. Praise the Lord!

Soon after I arrived, I met a Sierra Leonean in the market and we became friends. Although I knew little more than a few greetings in his language, I went with him to a remote village where he left me with his mother and five brothers. I stayed there for almost a month. I remember lying on the bed that first night thinking of the vast improbability of what I was doing. Here I was, lying on a bed of sticks and straw next to a man whose name I wasn't sure I would remember by the morning. I was a complete stranger among a people whose language I could not understand. I was miles away from the nearest hospital, with no transportation, in the heart of the country once known as "The White Man's Grave." Yet I was at peace because I had faith that the Lord had led me there and would take care of me.

In that village I began to grow "ears" for the language. Sounds began to take shape into syllables and words. I had no formal language helper, I made no recordings, but I was learning to communicate. Whenever I return to that village we recall my first days there. Interestingly enough, we remember a time of rich communication together!

I have now lived with three different people groups and have been learning three different languages. As the years have passed I have become friend and family to many people. My advice is sought concerning a marriage prospect. I may be part of the groom's family delegation to arrange bride price with the bride's family. I may be called to settle domestic quarrels. Even without being aware of it I have begun to have an insider's perspective and an insider's role.

A missionary friend invited me to say a few words to a group of village men one evening. It was an informal gathering of the church late at night under the stars. We were seated in a circle as if around a fire, but no fire was needed that evening because the night was sweet and warm. As I began to speak my friend nudged me, "Stand up! You are supposed to stand up when speaking!" When I voiced my disagreement, a Sierra Leonean man who had come with us was called in to settle the matter: "Shouldn't he stand up?" The reply: "Oh, by all means. And he must hold a book in his hand this way." He then gave an excellent imitation of the "missionary stance!" We were being shown how to play "missionary."

One of my closest African friends once asked me, "When these missionaries return home on leave, are they sent to a school where they are taught how to behave?" I was curious to know why he was asking the question. "Well," he replied, "when they first come here they act as if they have come just to please themselves. In fact, it is sometimes hard to believe they are even Christians. But each time they go on leave and come back they behave better." I told him that we are all constantly learning the proper way to behave here and that after a leave we just try harder!

I happen to know some of the people that this friend was referring to. They are fine Christians — dedicated, sacrificial, and hard working. Yet they have made some dreadful cultural blunders and do so constantly without seeming to be aware of it. They are not communicating a Christian witness. Clearly, *good intentions alone* are no guarantee of successful communication of the Christian Gospel — that takes spending time with the people, and developing personal ties with them.

In the past three years I have learned three African languages to various levels of proficiency. Two of these are fairly difficult tonal languages. (A little understatement there!) I have a proverb (these are very popular here in Africa):

> One excuse for not learning is as good as another.
> But those who learn the language have overcome every obstacle.

It is not surprising that Satan will do all that he can to discourage the Lord's people from being able to communicate the Gospel effectively and powerfully. How many times have I heard the Enemy scream into my ear, "You will never learn this language! Give up! You are not a competent linguist. You are out of your depth. Leave it for someone else!"

But, "I am confident that since the Lord has called me to this ministry he has equipped me for the task. My season to speak this language *will come,* for the Lord has said, 'He (that's *me!*) is like a tree planted by streams of water, which yields its fruit in season…' (Psalm 1:3). And, after all, if the ass could learn to speak Balaam's language in a day, I ought to be able to learn this language in three years!"

One of the difficulties I have had to overcome has been that I have not been able to find a steady language helper. But I am gaining skills at converting people in the community into language helpers on the spot. "Differential drills" are great for drawing people's attention to my desire for accuracy. And these are fun for everyone. While sitting in a smoky farm house as the women are preparing a meal, I will begin making digging motions with my hand and say the word for *hoe*. Then I will begin wiggling my arm and say the word for *snake*. They soon catch on to what I'm after. "Why I declare! Those words *are* very much alike aren't they?" Then they say the words while I act them out. I then do this with several other pairs of words. Some people even give me other sound-alikes!

I have found it difficult to get people to repeat a new word more than once. So when I hear a new word, I try to think of another word that sounds something like it. Then I do an impromptu differential drill on the spot. Neat trick! As I show my interest in these "small points," I see that people are much more apt to correct my mistakes.

I have collected various differential pairs, and I sometimes find a way to combine them into tricky sentences. I call these sentences *Tone Twisters* because one has to get the intonation correct in order to make sense. People have shown great interest in these tone twisters because of various classical tongue twisters in their language. I am showing interest in a cultural art form!

I also discovered that I could use the natural responses of the people in the community to show me my mistakes. For example, I know I have made a mistake if they say, *"Mmmm?"* (rising intonation), if they just stare blankly, if they get the giggles, if they call others around and say, "Would you repeat what you just said?" or if they say, "This language is sure tough for you, isn't it?"

Whenever this happens, I try to remember what I said so I can write it down and find out what I said wrong. Then I try again. One word that I have been struggling to say correctly is the word for "housefly." Using the principle "Learn a little and use it a lot," I try to work the word into various conversations. One of my friends has caught my apparent interest in flies and has suggested we write a book entitled *1001 Ways to Kill a Housefly!* (Would its sequel be *1001 Ways to Use Dead Flies!*?)

Progress in learning these languages has been slow and painful. Once when I was very discouraged, I went out under a mango tree near the village to pray. As I bowed my head, my eye caught sight of a little bean-like plant that had recently germinated. I knew immediately that the Lord was telling me something through that little plant: "As the first pair of leaves of this plant are grotesque and bear little resemblance to the parent plant, so it is with your first attempts to speak this language. But these leaves will soon be replaced by others more beautifully shaped. So it will be with you. Don't get discouraged!"

Another time after an especially difficult day, a man found me sitting by myself on a fallen tree. He took a look at me and then sat down beside me. After a few moments of silence he asked me, "Are you thinking of home?"

"I-want-to-speak-your-language," I replied haltingly.

"You will," he reflected. At that moment he had grasped the intensity of my desire to speak his language, and a bond was formed between us that has made us especially close.

I suppose I might have given up many times except for my belief that God will see me through to the completion of the task. I have a strong love for these people who do not know the Gospel, and this encourages me to keep on trying. Even when I make grammatical blunders, or when I am not sure what to say, I know that something *is* being communicated just by my being there where they are. May the Lord speed the day when my tongue will be free to speak all that my heart desires to say! On that day perhaps they will say: "But that is what we have always understood you to be saying!" ◊

She Kissed Me

She Kissed Me

by Jeanette Chaffee

I was in a hurry.
Tired.
But she called me.
Halfway up the 59 stairs to my house.
"Jacqueline, Jacqueline"
(that's what the apartment kids call me).
I'm glad I stopped.
I almost didn't.
Without a word
she reached up
and kissed me on the cheek.
The preciousness
of 30–second greetings
with a 7–year–old.

David Owen has captured seven vivid snapshots of the lives of Arab families. These pictures let us see not only the families but, more importantly, the journey that he and his wife, Sarah, have travelled in the process of learning and ministry.

David was a participant in the first language learning course we taught at the School of World Mission, back in 1976. He was learning Arabic with his Saudi friend, Abu Ru'a, and on various occasions it was our privilege to attend the LA mosque with David and Sarah. We will always remember our final class session, attended by the learners and their guests — their helpers from ethnic communities, many of whom were Muslim. David recited in Islamic style one of the Qur'anic Suras. It was a moving and enthusiastically–received recitation.

David is currently working on Al-Mushria, a Bible translation project in Islamic–style Arabic.

A few years ago we wrote a small booklet called Bonding and the Missionary Task. *Bonding was described as "establishing a sense of belonging" or "becoming a belonger" with the people of the new culture. Various of our contributors have used the term Bonding, and now David Owen organizes his chapter around the theme of families they have bonded with.*

Abu Banat — Father of Daughters

By David Owen

Every Arab family wants sons. Having a son is a very important part of traditional culture in the Middle East. They are what the family glories in. As they grow up they form the fortress that makes the family proud and strong. Sons are a sign of God's blessing to the parents, therefore every missionary couple working in the Arab East usually hopes and prays, at one time or another, for sons also. After all, if sons are such an important sign of God's blessing in traditional Arab culture, would not God, who is sending the missionary as a cross–cultural communicator, be more than ready to answer such a prayer?

But we, David and Sarah Owen, have three daughters. Among the Palestinian Arabs with whom we work, the father and the mother are called after the name of their oldest son. If your oldest son's name is *Khalid*, the father is known as *Abu Khalid* (the father of Khalid), and the mother is called *Im Khalid* (mother of Khalid). If you are one of the few families who have no sons, and they are rare, the father can be labeled *Abu Banat,* "Father of daughters," a very humiliating address. But usually the family continues to expand until a son arrives — one family in our Arab village had 11 daughters by the first wife and three more by a second wife until a son came! Fortunately, our Arab neighbors were kind to Sarah and me and usually called us

Abu and Im Melody, after our oldest daughter, although *Abu Banat* was said jokingly on several occasions.

Our sonless state has been harder on Sarah than on me. Birth and children are an important part of the conversation in women's circles. So Sarah has had to confront the problem more frequently than I. But we have found that as our girls grow up and do well in home and school they are a glory to God that people can see, and the talk usually simmers down. But, being "parent of daughters" was initially a major problem in our attempt to have an incarnational ministry among Palestinian Arabs in the Jerusalem area and was the topic of many of our early language learning experiences. As our story unfolds we will share some of the specific ways in which we have made up for that particular weakness in our lives.

We would like to hang our language learning experiences around our interaction with seven Arab families that we have formed belonging relationships — bonded with — over the past twelve years. These families were chosen because of their different roles in the Arab community, and they illustrate some of the varied ways one can interact with the community.

We have identified all of the families by a daughter, to protect their identity, but to also parallel our own family's situation. Therefore, when we speak of *Abu Nadia,* we are speaking of a father who has three sons and two daughters, one of whom is Nadia. After all, as many Arab families have told us in consolation, *"Alyom, albint zay alwalad"* — Today a daughter is the same as a son.

ABU RUTH — BONDING WITH AN ARAB IMMIGRANT TO AMERICA

Abu Ruth was a Lebanese Christian Arab who had married an American woman while in a Bible school in the

United States. He then went back to Lebanon to start a small evangelical church and Bible school in Beirut. Our relationship with Abu Ruth's family began at a time when they were back in the U.S. — the same year we began seriously considering working in the Arab world. Although he was an immigrant to the United States, Abu Ruth still had roots in Lebanon with plans for returning to minister there in the future. We were invited to their Los Angeles home for our first Arabic meal and there we learned our first Arabic words and phrases.

Our families became deep friends, and we were touched with the Middle East. It was that simple. They encouraged us to return with them and study Arabic at a small language school in Amman, Jordan. We could fly to Beirut and they would meet us at the airport and take us in for a while and then they would send us on to Amman.

That indeed turned out to be the beginning of our work in the Middle East. They met us in Lebanon and facilitated our arrival. The combination of Arab and American hospitality was perfect for our situation. They kept up with us throughout our year at language school in Amman, visiting us and allowing us to spend Christmas and several other occasions with them in Beirut.

It bothered many people, including our parents, members of our home churches and some supporting friends, that we chose an immigrant family as a vehicle to come to the Arab world, instead of a well–established mission board, which would provide more security for Sarah and me and our seven–month old daughter Melody. But this was the way we began our incarnational–style ministry — bonding with a Lebanese family.

Although our relationship with Abu Ruth's family has become somewhat distant over the years, God used them in our lives to get us started.

ABU RU'A — BONDING WITH AN ARAB STUDENT IN AMERICA

We were standing in the living room of a friend in Los Angeles who had a ministry to international students. There before us, with his obviously pregnant wife, was Abu Ru'a, a nervous, quick–speaking Saudi Arabian. As we greeted them, they were somewhat surprised by our modest Arabic which we had picked up in our year of language study in Amman. We began to relax over tea and listen to their story. Abu Ru'a was in his second year of graduate school. Over the Christmas holiday he returned home to Saudi Arabia, where he had been forced to marry a young girl from his family, and now they were expecting their first child. He was doing poorly at school since his return with his bride, and resented having this addition to his life. Im Ru'a, his shy wife, knew very little English. She was expecting in four months and was far away from her mother and sisters, who would normally have given support to her during pregnancy and childbirth. The college administration had contacted our student–worker friend to see if she could help the young family, and in turn she had contacted us, knowing that we had recently returned home from our language study in Jordan.

The previous year in Amman, the Jordanian community we had found ourselves in consisted almost entirely of Christian Arabs — although the Christians were only a 10 percent minority in a country that was 90 percent Muslim. Our Christian Arab friends had discouraged us from contact with Muslims, saying that such involvement for evangelistic reasons was either too dangerous or simply not fruitful. But now, in Los Angeles, we were on the brink of a relationship with a Muslim family from Mecca, Saudi Arabia. We immediately invited them over for dinner and an evening together at our home. They reciprocated and

God used this relationship to open the doors for us as missionaries to the Muslim world.

Their first need was for help as expectant parents. Sarah was able to be an older sister to Im Ru'a and encourage her to get ready for the event. But Ru'a's birth slipped up on us. They did not let us know when labor began, nor even of the baby's arrival. We had not heard from them for a suspiciously long time, so I called them on the telephone. Abu Ru'a answered, and I had to pull the news out of him. His wife had given birth to a *girl,* Ru'a — and they were both deeply disappointed. I asked if we could come see the newborn, and his response was to plead with us to come and take her away! Im Ru'a described to us her feelings of wanting to just throw the baby away. It was not that she disliked motherhood, but she was disappointed in having a girl, and she felt so cut off and alone in Los Angeles. In the following months our regular visits to their home were a comfort to them and opened the way to learn more about Saudi life.

I spent many late nights helping Abu Ru'a with math problems related to his major in education — with Turkish coffee keeping us awake. At the same time, I decided to begin my interaction with him on a spiritual plane by getting him to teach me how to read, in Islamic style, the short chapters at the end of the Arabic Qur'an. Eventually I also learned how to recite and perform the entire Islamic prayer routine.

I learned from Abu Ru'a not only what the prayers were, but also what they meant to him personally. I would ask him, "What is actually going on in your mind and heart when you say, *'Subhana rabbi l'ala,'* as your head touches the floor?" I also would ask myself, "Is he worshipping idolatrously? Or is *Allah* the God of the Bible as well?" We studied the passages in the Qur'an about Jesus and eventually began reading the Bible together. I began attending a regular Friday mosque service in Los Angeles with Abu Ru'a to pray with him and his Muslim friends.

Abu Ru'a introduced me to many of his Saudi friends and soon I had more contacts than I could possibly follow up. My Arabic was improving. I had open and friendly relationships with Muslims that could never have developed in a strict Muslim community overseas. Then one evening at Abu Ru'a's home we were introduced to a Palestinian Muslim couple from Be'er Sheva. That evening foretold of God's next phase for our ministry.

ABU AMAL — BONDING WITH OUR NEIGHBORS

We next found ourselves in an entirely Muslim village just east of Jerusalem. There we met Abu Amal, a friendly, outgoing person. He owned the house that seemed to be best for us in the village. It was a duplex. He and his family lived on one side and we on the other. In a sense, we were all in the same house, and this was our first real opportunity to live closely with a Muslim family. We found the neighbor–landlord situation to be a good way to establish a relationship in the community.

Abu Amal had three sons and two daughters. His mother lived with them. Several years before he had built the side of the duplex we were renting, in order to accommodate a second wife. She had lived there for several years, but Im Amal never accepted the arrangement, and the second wife was forced to leave.

We had no written contract for renting, just an agreement for a monthly sum which included water. After one year he wanted to begin to charge for water, but with some friendly negotiations that was settled in our favor. The fact that we had a financial relationship with Abu Amal never kept us from having an open neighborly friendship.

By that time we had a second daughter, Salima, and a newborn, Yasmin. Abu Amal's youngest daughter was a tremendous help to Sarah during those days when three children were too much. Their younger daughter often stayed on our side of the duplex and carried Yasmin around and entertained our other two daughters and helped them with their schoolwork too. Im Amal gave Sarah her first lessons in Arabic cooking. Our two kitchens were right next to each other, the two doors opening side by side. Abu Amal's mother hand–embroidered a Palestinian dress for Sarah, and she wore it on a number of occasions to Arab wedding parties in the village. Im Amal knew no English so Sarah was forced to converse with her in Arabic at all times.

My interaction with Abu Amal consisted mainly in sitting on his jasmine–covered veranda in the Spring and Summer, or in front of an olivewood–burning stove in the Winter, sipping tea or coffee, discussing two subjects — religion and politics. Abu Amal and his two sons did not pray five times a day or fast during Ramadan. Nevertheless, they were quite tough on theological elements of Islam: one God, belief in prophets, and the polemic stance against Christianity — rejecting the incarnation. To them it was impossible to conceive of Almighty God taking on a limited human form, and if he had, utterly foolish for him to be defeated on a cross — whether resurrected or not. I tried to emphasize to them the need for atonement — Muslims *do* sacrifice once a year on *Id el–adha,* the Feast of Sacrifice. I simply said that Jesus is our *adha.* How straightforward can you be?

Abu Amal and I always talked in Arabic. He knew a little English, but was too unsure of it to use it. His oldest son, who graduated first in his high school class, knew English quite well, and I often had a battle keeping the conversation in Arabic with him. Right in the middle of a sentence he would switch from Arabic to English! I would just have to sit tight in the conversation for several minutes — he still in English, while I in Arabic. Eventually he would get the point; I wasn't budging. I found the best way to get out of the problem, was just to say, "I promise that if you ever come to visit us in America, we will speak English with you. In the meantime, please let us speak Arabic!"

ABU IBTISAM — BONDING THROUGH RELATIONSHIPS BUILT BY OUR CHILDREN

"Allah razaqna bitalat banat," (God has blessed us with three daughters) we told our friends in the Muslim village over and over again.

But what about schooling? After much investigation and prayer, we put our first two children in a Muslim–Arabic school. It was a combination Kindergarten–First Grade private school on the top of the Mount of Olives. A school bus came to our village and picked them up at 7:30 a.m. and returned them about 1:00 p.m. Melody and Salima were the only Christians or foreigners to attend among the 200 students. Many Christian missionary friends in the area advised us against it. Their reasons were: poor–quality Arab curriculum, the Islamic religious atmosphere, and fear that they would forget their mother tongue! One missionary even dared to warn us that if they grew up attending *Arabic* schools they would never be able to attend a certain Ivy League University!

Melody was plunged into Kindergarten. For about two weeks we weren't sure she would make it, but she did. Within six weeks she was speaking Arabic well. What a miracle it seemed to us adults, struggling with language learning. But the secret was really no secret. If we, even as adults, would plunge ourselves into an intense situation for six hours every day where we were forced to interact in the new language, we would pick it up quickly too. But as adults we would rather maintain our distance from people and we prefer the gradual approach. For the two years Melody was attending the Islamic school she memorized Muslim prayers and long Qur'anic passages. It did get heavy at times. At bedtime we would often re-explain to Melody the purpose of our presence in the Arab world, and go over the difference between the Qur'an and the Bible and the essentials of our faith in Jesus. We believe the whole experience gave her a special insight and love for Muslims that few Christian children ever receive.

Melody quickly bonded with a Muslim classmate named Ibtisam, from another part of our village. They especially enjoyed doing homework together at Ibtisam's house. It was an intense relationship that made life fun for Melody. Ibtisam was the seventh and last child, the only daughter. Her name means "Smiling." We soon met Abu Ibtisam and his wife, who were very friendly people. They knew no English, which kept our conversation always in Arabic. They were helpful in that they always addressed us at a moderate speed in Arabic, kept their vocabulary simple, and enunciated very clearly. We had never known another family like them.

Abu Ibtisam, a humble cook at a Jerusalem restaurant, was fairly poor. He was quite open in telling me about his faith, but eager to hear about my work in Bible translation in Arabic. Im Ibtisam was a bit defensive, very regular in prayers, and often publicly corrective of her husband if he showed too much interest in what we were doing. But we did become close friends with the family through Melody's friendship, which would have never happened if we had sent her to the Anglican–English school in West Jerusalem.

In order to keep up our simple lifestyle without a car, we eventually chose to move into the old city of Jerusalem, and to send our children to an evangelical Lutheran Arabic school so the girls could walk to school. Three–fourths of the students are Christian Arabs and one fourth are Muslim.

Melody is now in the sixth grade, Salima in the third and Yasmin in the first grade. All are doing well, always at the top of their classes and emotionally stable, too. We still speak some English in our home to keep the language alive for them, and we have a series of supplementary books in English which we use with them at home. The whole experience with the girls in Arabic schools has been a blessing for us and has brought us into belonging relationships with folks in the community. In fact, we consider our decision to have our children in Arabic school to be the single most significant factor in our acceptance by the Arab community.

Helping our children with their Arabic homework from the beginning has been great for our Arabic as well. Since I have followed Melody in her lessons, I know for certain that I am now on at least a sixth grade level! Sometimes it is hard to accept the fact that Saladin is my child's hero of history, instead of George Washington, but that is a part of belonging also. There was a time, early in our language learning, when we thought it would be great to have an Arab living with us in our home to help us learn Arabic faster. But we soon found that unnecessary, for now we have three native speakers living with us, our daughters.

ABU MUFIDA — BONDING THROUGH THE COMMUNITY GROCER

I was in the United States recently, to be in touch with some of our supporters. One of them took me out to eat one evening and dropped what I could tell was a premeditated question. "David, have you in your experience with Muslims ever run across a seemingly righteous man, who was faithful to Islam and seemed to have a lifestyle that paralleled the best Christian you have seen?"

My answer came immediately. "Yes, Abu Mufida." He was our grocer in the Muslim village. He had a tidy, small shop about a five–minute walk from our house, and was fairly well off materially. Abu Mufida spoke only Arabic, he was sixty–five years old and had been running a shop in almost the same location for forty–five years. We bought from him lentils, milk, yogurt, cheese, school supplies for our children and a crusty bread called *Qarshelli* that we ate for for breakfast with milk. We saw him almost every day. Abu Mufida was the unofficial head of his clan, and people came to settle their disputes with him. I listened to a number of cases settled in the living room of his house, next door to his shop. He had the reputation of being scrupulously honest and fair, even the occupation army admired and respected him. One person said of Abu Mufida, "He speaks the same word to everyone whether rich or poor, important or insignificant, Arab or Jew."

He was very faithful in his prayers, never missing a single one. I took him with me on a trip to Galilee once and when it was time for the noon prayer he became restless. "*Dawood* (David)," he said, "We must find a mosque." We did and he prayed. He always fasted the month of Ramadan with a washed face, combed hair and a smile, and always said toward the end of the month, "If only Ramadan lasted the whole year!" Once, in the summer, I entered his store after a hot day in Jerusalem. He gave me a chair and sent a grandchild to bring me some tea and grapes. The child returned with some of the largest, most beautiful grapes I've ever seen. I asked Abu Mufida if these were from his vineyard. He said, "Yes." I asked him what his secret was, why were they so superior to all the grapes around? "The secret is simple," he said, "Prayer and fasting!"

Abu Mufida lived with his wife and one married son. He had six grown children. The situation with his older son was the only seemingly hurting point in his life. This son was a leader in the Palestinian resistance movement in Syria and therefore forbidden by Israel to ever return home again, nor would Israel allow Abu Mufida to leave and visit his son. They had not seen each other for over ten years. He was proud of his son's cause, but heartsick over the separation. I prayed with Abu Mufida about the situation a number of times. He seemed almost to accept me as a son in place of the separated one. As the clan leader, his acceptance of me and my family was important protection for us in our ministry in the area.

Sarah became good friends with his daughter–in–law, who lived with them. She was a young mother like Sarah and the relationship seemed to be mutually supportive. Sarah was able to pass on Christian magazines and Bibles for the family through this friendship. One day a Muslim Sheik in the clan came by their home and found a Bible, became absorbed in its contents and took it home to continue reading. He never returned it. Sarah gave them another to replace it.

There are modern grocery stores in Jerusalem with the latest western prepared foods. But we chose to shop in our village and this opened up the door for a bonding situation with the most influential family in a clan of over 2,000. Abu Mufida, and the members of his family have not yet come to a full knowledge of faith in Jesus, but we see God's hand in our relationship with them and believe that some day they will.

ABU NADIA — BONDING THROUGH THE STREET ENCOUNTER

In every ministry situation, there is always the chance encounter that proves valuable in the long run. Soon after moving into the Muslim village, I happened to strike up a conversation with an eighteen–year–old whose friendship led to another belonging relationship for our family.

He took me home and introduced me to his family. My new friend's father, Abu Nadia, was a refugee. He was born and raised in Jaffa, but was forced from his home in 1948 and he settled in this village outside of Jerusalem to raise his family. Each of the three Arab clans in our village sticks to itself socially, and any Arab who moves into the village is always considered somewhat of an outsider. This was Abu Nadia's situation, even after thirty years, despite the fact that he too was a Palestinian Arab. Besides that, he had married a Lebanese wife. The Lebanese are significantly different culturally from the Palestinians, so Abu Nadia's five children had severe adjustments to make socially as they were growing up. They were almost considered as outcasts.

Their family was very open to our family and loved to talk. They were seekers in the real sense of the word since their social situation had molded them into that role.

But Abu Nadia did want something specific from our relationship that caused a problem. His oldest son, whom I had met on the bus, was doing very poorly in his last year of high school in the required subject of English. He probably would not pass his final exams to graduate. Abu Nadia wanted me to tutor his son. I refused and refused. I had determined before we came to the village that I would not be forced into the role of English teacher. If I allowed that to happen, everybody would know me as such and be practicing English with me whenever I was around. I still had far to go in my own learning of Arabic.

My friend failed his exams and had to repeat his senior year at his father's expense. There was a general feeling from the family that I could have made a difference. It was a difficult situation. English teaching is especially appreciated here where one–third of the final high school exam is in English, but that wasn't my calling and I stood firm in my commitment to be known as an Arabic speaker.

Our relationship with Abu Nadia has continued to be warm nevertheless, and we have broken many Ramadan fasts together, sitting on the floor of their kitchen with a glass of licorice juice in our hands, waiting for the evening call to prayer from Aqsa mosque to signal the break of the fast. We have taken trips together, and studied the sample chapters of our translation project as they came out. Recently while we were in America, one of Abu Nadia's daughters who was studying nursing in America came and visited us for a week–end, and worshipped with us in our home Presbyterian Church. It has been a great example of a street encounter that led to a belonging relationship.

ABU RAZAN — BONDING THROUGH A WORK RELATIONSHIP

One would probably expect that an on–going working relationship would be the best situation to be able to bond with the local community. I've found that to be true. For the last four years I have had a working relationship with a well–known Palestinian poet from a Jerusalem Muslim family. He is a few years older than I, but we are close enough to be near equals. Abu Razan is my translation partner. I deal with the translation and exegetical problems from the Biblical text and he is the stylist in literary Arabic. We were introduced to one another by a mutual friend who knew us individually and realized that we had similar aspirations for Bible translation in Arabic.

Abu Razan loves the Arabic language with a passion. For the most part, all of our conversations are in Arabic, often in a semi-classical style since he is a teacher. He only speaks English with me when he feels someone is eavesdropping on his telephone line or when his parents are in the room and he does not want them to know the details of our work. (Abu Razan's father is a *hajj*, a pilgrim to Mecca.) I have benefited greatly from my four years of relating to Abu Razan through our work. And my greatest advances in speaking and reading Arabic have come through our relationship. As we have worked on our Bible translation project, we have discussed all aspects of faith in Jesus and what they might mean for the Muslim community. We have discovered redemptive analogies together in Islam that will be key theological stepping stones in our Bible translation project for Muslim readers.

When I met Abu Razan four years ago, he was a Bible–reading Muslim, but unsettled in his understanding of the cross. Today he is a Messianic Muslim, trusting in Jesus' sacrificial blood for his salvation. Our working relationship has been the means for his fuller understanding of the faith.

Abu Razan has four daughters and no sons. This is another common element of our shared life. There are signs that his wife is growing in faith also. The secretary of our translation project, Alice Hall, has related regularly with Im Razan, as a personal friend and is helping to cultivate her faith.

I expected Abu Razan to come and work with me in the research center at Bethlehem where we first had our office, but he refused, saying that he did not like the academic atmosphere of the place. He would only work with me in the living room of his home in the Muslim neighborhood where he lives. This irritated me for a while because it is often hard to concentrate with children, a wife, relatives, and a mother–in–law in the same room. But his insistence has kept me in an Arab home, forced me into conversation with his family and the neighbors, and has kept my Arabic at an even higher plane. Being flexible has been a principle that has paid off many times in relationships in the Middle East, the fruits of which have often been new opportunities for language learning and ministry.

◊

Incarnational Living
by Hudson Taylor

The Incarnation shows that, provided we keep from sin, we cannot go too far in meeting this people and getting to know them, getting to be one with them, getting into sympathy with them.

There is wonderful instruction in the way in which the Lord Jesus wrought His works of mercy. He *touched* the leper and the blind when He healed them. The woman felt that if she only touched the hem of His garment she would be sure to be healed; and the Saviour felt that virtue had gone out of Him. If we keep so far from the people that they cannot even touch the hem of our garment, how will virtue go out of us? Sometimes they are not clean, and we are tempted to draw our skirts together; but I believe there is no blessing when this is the case. Contact is a real power that we may use for God.

We are to *manifest* the truth, as well as preach it. We tell people that the world is vain; let our lives *manifest* that this is so. We tell them that our Home is above, does our dwelling look like it? Oh, to live consistent lives.

It is not preaching only that will do what needs to be done. Our life must be one of visible self-sacrifice. There is much sacrifice in our lives of which the Chinese cannot know. God knows all about it, and we can well afford to wait His declaration of it and His award. There is much we have left for the sake of the Chinese which they have never seen. That will not suffice. They must *see self-sacrifice* in things they cannot but understand.[1]

---

[1]From Hudson Taylor, in ***Hudson Taylor and the China Inland Mission***, by Dr. & Mrs. Howard Taylor, China Inland Mission, London, 1918, pp 405-406.

At the time we wrote BONDING AND THE MISSIONARY TASK *we expressed a pessimism about the ability of established missionaries to change their lifestyles and become deeply bonded with the people. However, in the last half–dozen years the many reports of people who have implemented a course of action that enabled them to establish belonging relationships have caused us to revise our pessimism.*

Koos and Anneleen Louw are an example of a couple who have now experienced bonding after twenty–three years of missionary service. In their case, they relocated to a new people group with a new language. Most cases of successful belated bonding that we are familiar with have been the result of a relocation, though many have done so within the same language.

This past year we held a workshop for language educators, at UNISA (University of South Africa in Pretoria). It was fun having Anneleen there to share her experience. Her joy was contagious as she described how she and her husband have been "rejuvenated" through the new perspectives and relationships that they have gained by living with the Swazi people.

My Belated Bonding

by Anneleen Louw

I grew up in a parsonage in Johannesburg, South Africa, with only white Afrikaans people around me. For us, apartheid was the natural way of living.

For more than 20 years my husband, Koos, and our four sons and I were missionaries to the Northern Sotho people of South Africa. But we lived in a "white island" community and we only left this "island" to take the gospel message to the "other" people. Then we would return to the comfort of our home, our language and our people. Deep in my heart I was always glad that I could bring the gospel to the Sotho people, but I was also glad that it was not necessary for me to become too deeply involved with them. For more than twenty years our ministry consisted primarily of forays out to the people.

Then in 1981 my husband attended a Language & Culture Learning course taught by Tom and Betty Sue Brewster in Hammanskraal. After the course I read the *LAMP* book and the other course materials, and shortly thereafter we had an opportunity for a change of ministry location.

We began to realize that, through ignorance, we had lived and worked as non-bonded missionaries for 23 years, blindly following the example of our predecessors. But after reading *Bonding and the Missionary Task,* our perspectives were radically changed. Although I could not see how it would work out practically in our situation, the Lord took over by giving us a new country and a new language where we could apply bonding principles and make a midlife adjustment of our lifestyle. The Lord was calling us to Swaziland.

All our children were already out of the house, and we as a couple were back where we started — doing everything together. We were ready to tackle together a new adventure, in a new country, to learn a new language and to start a belated bonding experience. The anticipation came as a fresh breeze and made us feel years younger.

A NEW START, PREJUDICE BEGINS TO FALL

Swaziland is a country with no apartheid laws, where we were to find that these black people are not afraid of white people, nor do they feel inferior to whites.

For our language learning time we went to a farming area, where for two months we lived with our Swazi helpers. Amos and Immaculate Makhunga are both lovable and open, exceptionally friendly and with good humor — laughing heartily and easily. They live very simply in a four–room *rondavel* (oval thatched house) with a coal stove and a minimum of furniture. We came into their home with a will to live as they do. By living with them we were accepted as part of their family and not treated as guests. We helped with the cooking, washing, and kindling the fire.

That was a real breakthrough for us. According to our Afrikaans culture we were not supposed to mix socially with black people — and here we were living with them.

After only six days we reached a minor milestone in the language — at dinner time we noted that we knew the names of everything on the table in SiSwati, and not a word of English was spoken during the whole meal, only SiSwati! A real triumph!

A very close relationship developed between us. They became our friends and treated us as equals. They taught us to speak SiSwati, to eat the same food they did, do the same things they did, and live the way they did. They were active Christians and we could share in the Lord.

Each day Immaculate Makhunga and I fetched water at the river. Pail in hand, I would carry it back to the house, swopping it over from one hand to the other. I had earlier said to her, "I can't carry it on my head." She didn't make any comment.

About a week later, one afternoon there at the river she placed a little folded rag on my head and simply said, "It's easy," as she lifted the pail onto my head. I got a firm grip on the pail with both hands, and then I had to follow her up the steep hill, stepping from rock to rock. Water showered my face and shoulders and I was soaked — but I reached the top! Koos had heard our laughing and shouting, and he ran to get the camera so that the event could be recorded on film for posterity.

At first I felt degraded, since my association with water–carrying had been that it was what only black people do. But then the realization came that by carrying water on my head I was giving something of myself and becoming one with them. That brought a warm feeling of satisfaction and belonging. I was experiencing that black people are human beings just as we are but with other habits and ways of doing things. My prejudices were breaking down.

That was also the beginning of easier water–fetching. I discovered that on my head it's not so heavy — the load is evenly divided.

On another occasion in that first week, while washing our clothes at the river the current carried my only bar of soap away. I went chasing after it, unsuccessfully — after that I learned how *they* hold the soap when washing at the river. My helper told me how to talk about this experience in SiSwati, and then we went round to see our friends and she kept saying, "Tell them about the soap!...Tell them about the soap!" My story brought much laughter to our community and through this experience I made many friends.

We were beginning to experience belonging relationships with the people who lived in our neighborhood. One said, "I like it that you visit us on foot and not by car."

THE WOMAN LEARNER

At first, Koos and I and the Makhungas went everywhere together, visiting people and speaking SiSwati. But I found that since I was a woman I did not get as many chances to speak. The men speak, and women must listen. Immaculate Makhunga and I soon decided to go visiting alone. That opened a new era to me.

Now I could talk and ask questions freely and we could talk about women's things. It is more natural for a woman to move among women and children. We have so much in common, so much to share and we can do things together. A housewife is a housewife in every culture.

Shortly after we arrived, Immaculate became ill and I had to take over the housekeeping: washing, cooking and cleaning, fetching water, etc. When other women came to visit the patient, they saw that I was now the housewife. They helped me by bringing vegetables and water to the house, and they started to teach me the Swazi way.

On another occasion, an old woman invited me to her humble kitchen. In no way did she excuse herself or her kitchen for being primitive or inferior. There in that wooden shack she taught me to grind mealies and then to make bread out of it. She could only speak SiSwati. How much I learned that morning!

NEW FREEDOMS

I was experiencing a deep change of feeling, from the prejudices of my background to new freedom in relationships with black people. Separation between races had been a natural and unquestioned way of living. Like many others from my country I had assumed that black people were essentially ignorant and inferior. But now, my mind was opened to meet black people who accepted me as an equal. And, even more significantly, I accepted them and needed them. I was dependent on them. They knew more than I. My attitudes and my way of thinking completely changed.

For 23 years I had been the white missionary who had come to share my knowledge and my care. I thought I understood them. I would go into their huts and greet them and drink their tea. I did love them, but I was not bonded with them. I was still a privileged outsider. I was still given their best, the chair, the best cup ...

Now, I am just one of them. I sit flat on the floor in the circle with others, dipping my hand into the same dish and eating the same food they eat. I sit in church next to them, not separately. I am a belonger.

Previously I was willing to shake hands formally, but now I can really take a black person's hand with both of mine and shake it heartily to communicate my real joy in seeing my friend. And we can hug each other, with none of the feelings that I had held before that this was not decent behavior for a white person.

We also learned to be more sensitive in the way we addressed people. When we lived in South Africa, it was customary for the whites to address any black man or woman by their first name — even if they were older than we. But now we realize that calling someone by his or her surname (especially saying "Mr." or "Mrs.") is the highest form of respect. And it now comes naturally and easily to greet our friends this way.

FROM PREJUDICE TO FREEDOM

Prejudice is a problem which stands in the way of bonding. For us, prejudice was the result of the established way of contact between the races, and of the education we received at home and at school. This background made prejudice a part of us and we were even blind to the fact that we were prejudiced.

Personally I was unaware of the racial prejudice that ruled my life. But learning the language through relationships has freed me, and enabled me to both receive and give acceptance in our new black community. These insights have come belatedly into our lives, but we thank God for this way of communicating the love of Jesus as we minister to the people.

Now we have our own home among the Swazis, with no white neighbors. The fact that our house is open day and night to anybody, has brought a freedom of life and spirit. People are coming and going all the time, and we are sharing everything.

The practical experience of becoming belongers with the Swazi people has changed my inner being and has drawn us into a deeper relationship with our Lord.

◊

One of the darkest nights we ever spent was a night a few years ago when we stayed with Doug and Robyn Priest in their Maasai home in the Loita Hills of Kenya. Lying in bed that night in their windowless structure we were impressed by the almost absolute blackness. We had set aside a week to visit the field locations of various language learners of the Christian Missionary Fellowship in Kenya.

Originally, the CMF had concentrated their efforts in Ethiopia. After missionaries were expelled from Ethiopia, CMF sent their people to our Language/Culture Learning & Mission course prior to their reassignment. Since then, the entire mission has made a deep commitment to learning and relationships as a foundation for ministry. The mission demonstrates its commitment by making sure that all of its missionaries are well trained for language/culture learning, and that they are given time, opportunity and encouragement to carry out their learning. As a mission, CMF has chosen to work among tough languages — Maasai, Turkana, and Javanese. Even so, CMF people have gained a reputation of being among the better language users of any mission.

Doug and Robyn moved into a Maasai village to learn the language and get to know the people's ways. At one time the Maasai were considered to be a stoic and resistant people; nevertheless, the Priests have developed deep relationships with them. In recent years God's Spirit has been moving. During their first term the Lord blessed their work and, when they left for furlough, regular worship services were being held in five villages.

One of Doug's hobbies is collecting Maasai proverbs. He has one of the finest collections anywhere.

Unless You Become as One of These

---

by Doug and Robyn Priest

Ole Manangoi had four wives. He arranged for his youngest wife to move out of her house to make a place for us to live. We would pay a rental fee and would be allowed and encouraged to make modifications on the house. For the next year we lived in this village, with no running water, no electricity, a dirt floor, no car, no refrigerator and a host of field rats as house guests. Our improvements to the house consisted in first putting plastic and then cardboard on the walls to keep out the cold wind and later buying a plastic barrel to catch the rain for our water supply.

We arrived in Kenya in 1978 to work with the Maasai people. Our mission, the Christian Missionary Fellowship, believed in the importance of language and culture learning, and our first year was set aside with no formal ministry responsibilities — our sole goal for the entire year was to study the Maasai language and culture. To facilitate our language learning we chose to live in the "bush" in a fairly traditional Maasai village — the village of Ole Manangoi, a Maasai man whose entire family were church–goers.

Each day we practiced our drills and learned our texts in the morning. After lunch we would walk thirty minutes to the primary school and practice our texts on the many people we saw on the road and at the school. We would then meet with two of the teachers who were our language helpers. Following these discussions and gathering cultural data, we would return home in time to visit in our village and then cook supper. In the evenings we read, visited in the village, had the village children in our house or worked over the day's notes. On four occasions we spent a week at a mission station studying Maasai grammar with two ladies who had worked among the Maasai for twenty-five years.

◊ ***Robyn*** ◊ One of the things we tried very hard to do our first year in Kenya was to involve ourselves in the life of the local community. A mentor of ours was Ng'oto Leina, Ole Manangoi's first wife. She was a new Christian and was delighted that her husband's village was hosting us. We spent wonderful evenings of Christian fellowship in her small, dark and smoky home, singing songs, praying and learning. She taught me to milk a cow, and she also let me accompany her with the other village women on the long trip to the spring where the village got their water.

Ng'oto Leina continued to grow as a Christian and after we left her village we would see her occasionally at women's meetings in the district capital. Once while driving on a road near her village we saw her carrying water. We stopped to greet her. She dropped her load and came running toward us, shouting our names, hugging and even kissing us when she reached us. She called our new baby her granddaughter and told us that she had been praying for us since we had left her village to work with others of her tribe who had not yet heard about Jesus. We now understood the Maasai proverb, *"Melakua ang' inchu"* (Home is never far away when you are alive). Her home was our home — and always would be.

THE FIRST NAMING

◊ ***Robyn*** ◊ After we had lived in the village for about six months, Doug began to collect Maasai proverbs, riddles and stories. He spent so much time collecting, editing and typing these that I began to suspect that he was "wasting his time." A couple years later, however, when spending the night in a village with Doug, I was able to see how he used these communication forms in discussion and merriment around the fire and how they sometimes served as a basis for teaching. He would begin, "I know a story much like the one you have about the diviner who had the two sons who argued over the inheritance."

"Tell us about it."

"There once was an old man whose name was Isaac. He had two sons, named Jacob and Esau ...."

• **Doug** • We experienced many joys throughout our first year of living with the Maasai as we learned their language and culture, but we also faced some challenges. We got tired of living in a house that had a dirt floor and that was too cold because we had no fire in the middle of the house. We longed for warm soaking tub baths. We found ourselves wishing for our own house and anxious to begin the work of evangelism and church planting. We made mistakes in our dealings with the people and there were days we despaired of ever learning to sound like the Maasai. How true was the Maasai saying, *"Merisio inyuat o inkidamat"* (Effort and ability are not the same thing).

We wanted to have Maasai names, but we had no idea how this was customarily done, so we encouraged the villagers to name us. At the time, we were proud of these new names. My name was a name for men my age. But as we came to better understand the Maasai culture, to our chagrin we realized that men of my age group do not really command the respect necessary to speak in public gatherings. That respect comes only with age. I was also called "left–handed" — until I learned about the Maasai proverb that says, "War (trouble) always comes from the left." Furthermore, we had been named by a woman, but we learned that it was only the old men who were the ones to give names. Needless to say, when we moved from that area we left these Maasai names behind.

THE SECOND NAMING

• **Doug** • The Loita Hills area had no churches. The number of Christians among the nearly eight–thousand people was almost nil. Three men had become Christians while attending school some years before, and recently they had started attending Bible courses some three hours drive away. They asked for a missionary to come and live in their area to assist in evangelism and teaching. They provided sponsorship for us to come to the Loita Hills. So, during our second year in Kenya we moved to that area to begin our ministry of evangelism and church planting.

We found a small building that we could lease and remodel. One of the first items on our agenda was to be given new Maasai names. Our awareness of the culture had progressed somewhat, so we asked the elder of the sponsoring village to give us our names. In the early morning, after spending the night in his village, we were again named and were blessed by him. We were both given first names as well as the family name of the village.

This sponsorship was good for us in our first months as it served as an introduction wherever we went. Later we realized that we had become too closely linked with this family and in so doing were limiting our potential involvement with others. We were asked, "Why did you choose only this family? Why not be a part of our family?" We realized that though there were surely benefits to having a local family name, there were some disadvantages as well. We began to use our first names primarily, even though we knew that the Maasai are referred to by their family names and it is rude in Maasai custom to call someone by their first name.

The skills that we had gained during our year of language and culture learning allowed us to become rather quickly accepted by our new Loita Hills community. We spent a lot of time visiting villages to meet people and we came to be viewed as wanting to help the Maasai people.

◊ ***Robyn*** ◊ Children, along with cows, are the most important possession of the Maasai. Realizing this, and observing many of the customs surrounding birth, we began to ask questions about pregnancy, birth and naming practices. The information we gathered led us not only to a better cultural understanding but to some new areas of ministry. Learning that most Maasai women severely restrict their diet during the last months of pregnancy, I began informal discussions on prenatal health care. I had a ready hearing among the women, especially when they observed how I acted during my own pregnancy. I was able to show them that they did not need to starve themselves during the last months of their pregnancy, but that a stronger mother meant an easier delivery. Some of these same women began coming to the local church service because of our friendship. After the service we women would sit together and chat about our new children.

• **Doug** • My Maasai helper and I began to produce lesson materials which could be used for evangelism and teaching. These materials, interspersed with songs, prayers and sound effects, were recorded on tape and used in the Loita area with hand–operated tape recorders. Others on our mission team in Kenya shared in the process and together they produced and copied many tapes which were listened to in dozens of villages all over southern Kenya.

◊ ***Robyn*** ◊ About this time I experienced my first real plateau in language learning. We were spending a lot of time putting in ceilings and painting our leased house, and my pregnancy made me want to stay at home rather than walk to the villages, so more and more of my visiting was done in *our* house rather than in *Maasai* houses. But perhaps the real reason for the plateau was that I began to slip out of my learner role. Being fluent in the language, I began to listen less and became somewhat lazy in gaining new vocabulary. I quit asking as many questions about the things I was hearing but not understanding.

Doug's language learning did not slow down, primarily because of the amount of time he was working on preparing lessons, but his time in the villages became less and less. He found himself wanting to spend time in the office typing a lesson in Maasai rather than making the effort to get out into the villages to be with people. Fortunately for both of us, this period of retreat lasted only about six months.

THE THIRD NAMING

• **Doug** • Our last year and a half in Loita was the most fruitful of our entire first term. In the previous three years we had made good progress both in language learning and in understanding the Maasai culture. We had lived through what is commonly called "culture shock." We had many Maasai friends who had taught us and had been exceedingly patient with us at every phase of our development. We had discovered both our strengths and weaknesses and were beginning to function as church planters.

The turning point for this final part of our term came when we were invited to visit the village of Enkipang'asi, about fifteen miles away, to teach the villagers, who were anxious to learn. I left a tape player after my get–acquainted visit and promised that I would return in a couple of weeks. Upon my return I was pleased that many people from the village had learned the songs (primarily traditional Maasai tunes with new Christian words) and could answer questions about the messages on the tape.

I returned frequently to Enkipang'asi during the next eighteen months. A typical visit began in the afternoon with a cup or two of tea or sour milk followed by talking about what was happening with the livestock and discussing other noteworthy events. Afterwards the herds returned and the village people were busy with milking, securing the fences and separating the sheep and goats from the cattle. Darkness came, and after supper they would bring out the tape player, listen to several lessons, and have a time of singing and discussion. Prayers and another cup of tea before going to sleep at about eleven o'clock ended the day.

In the morning the people would gather around and listen to the next lesson, offering their comments and exhortations based on the lesson. Some of them later attended advanced two-week Bible courses which were held for the Maasai in another town.

Ole Maison, one of the men from Enkipang'asi, was learning to read and was leading his family and village in worship. It was he that encouraged his village to begin to collect poles and start putting up their own church building. He and I used to sit out underneath the sparse shade of a thorn tree and talk about what it meant to be a Christian and a Maasai.

"Can I be a Christian even if I have two wives?"

"Why not? Abraham had great faith in God and so did David."

"But I have heard that you cannot join some churches if you have more than one wife."

"That is true. Different churches have different rules. But I believe that God does not want married people to divorce — even if they are polygamous people."

◊ ***Robyn*** ◊ Children are of great value and importance to the Maasai, so having our first child while living among them gave us new opportunities for involvement. The Maasai had always questioned why we had been married for four years and yet had no children. When it became apparent that our first child was on her way, we became the objects of new interest, teasing and conversation. They watched me and commented on my behavior and eating habits in my new condition. My friends often shared the stories of their own childbirth experiences — greatly emphasizing the length and pain of their labor and delivery. My pregnancy gave me something very basic and real in common with the women. I used the occasion to share my faith by explaining that it was God who gave life and He is the Father of all people, and that He Himself had a Child.

When we returned home from the hospital with our new baby, Nicole, many delegations of Maasai women visited us. They came with gifts of milk, sugar and maize meal, just as I had done when visiting them after they had their babies. They all blessed our baby by spraying spittle on her, and each woman had some particular childcare advice to share. After a few months had passed we were ready to hold our first real Maasai celebration — our baby's naming ceremony where she would be given a Maasai name.

Doug bought a small ox to be slaughtered and roasted on the day of the feast. I purchased tea, sugar, flour and shortening to make the usual side dishes. The women of the village gathered firewood to assist us, and we invited the entire surrounding community to join with us in our celebration.

When the appropriate day came, the feast began. The men led the ox to the forest to be slaughtered and cooked. The women made tea. Visitors came bringing gifts of milk to be shared as needed. About two hundred people came to be part of the ceremony. Throughout the day we ate and visited. In the afternoon one of the local Christians gave a short message, followed by a brief time of prayer and as a community we gave thanks to God for being Creator and Father. Most of the people were not Christians, but all Maasai pray to God and acknowledge Him as Creator.

• **Doug** • In the evening after everyone had eaten their fill, the visitors left to return to their homes. We stayed at the village where the feast had been held. After the cows had been milked and enclosed for the night, the actual naming took place. Stools were brought for the older men and for both of us. All those present were given sodas to drink rather than the more usual honey beer. After a playful discussion in which the baby's attributes were mentioned, several names were suggested.

"We could call her *'Namunyak'* (Blessed One), because she has brought blessing to her parents."

"We could call her *'Nairrotiai'* (Where the Water Lies), because of the wide place in the stream by her house."

"Or we could call her *'Enentesekera'* (She who is from Entesekera), because that is where she lives."

"*'Neloita'* is a good name because she belongs to all of us who live in Loita."

Finally one of the older men said, "Let us give her the name that we have chosen for her." The elder of the village then addressed me four times as father of the child with a name that was *not* intended for the child. Each of the four times I was called, I ignored the man. Much laughter accompanied this "false" naming.

The elder then called out four times, *"Father of Nairrotiai."* Each time I responded, since this was the true name given to the child. The old man continued by giving his blessing to the baby:

> "May God bless your child. May she have brothers and sisters. May she live a long life. May she be blessed. May she have many cattle. May no unfortunate thing happen to her. May she prosper. May she one day have many children of her own. May she defeat her enemies."

At the end of each of these phrases, the entire group answered in unison, "Yes, my Lord (may it be so)." Several elders and older women repeated the entire process of naming the child and blessing both child and parents.

Tears filled our eyes and made it difficult for us to answer when we were supposed to respond. Rarely had we felt so close to our Maasai friends and so much a part of their lives. How thankful we were for their love and acceptance of us. The day of this third naming ceremony was one of reward and encouragement for us. It made all of the long struggle of language and culture learning eminently worthwhile. And from that day onward we were addressed in the usual Maasai form of "Mother of Nairrotiai" and "Father of Nairrotiai."

FRUIT FOR OUR LABORS

• **Doug** & ***Robyn*** • Looking back on our first term in Kenya we realize that the progress that we made in cultural identification and in ministry can in large part be directly traced to the effort we put into language and culture learning. We feel that without assuming the important role of learners we could not have begun to minister as effectively in the Loita Hills. We chose the role of learner and tried to keep that role even when it would have been easy to move in the direction of knower or teacher.

When we came to Loita there were but a handful of Christians. God blessed our efforts and those of the first Christians. When we left, five villages were having weekly worship services and other villages were at the point of beginning to hold worship services. A dozen people had been baptized, and nearly a hundred more were considering such a decision. We had a ready hearing and an open invitation to visit and teach in most areas.

We left the Loita Hills for furlough at a time when the traditional fruit of missionary work was just becoming measurable. After our return we once again visited the Loita Hills to visit our many friends, to see how the work was progressing, and to visit some of the villages that are meeting regularly for worship. We were very encouraged by many of the things that we saw.

The best news came from Enkipang'asi. Due to an extended drought in the area, many of the families from the village had moved in order to find water and grass. Nevertheless, they still came together whenever they could, to enjoy Christian fellowship and teaching. Their faith as a group was growing and many were anxiously awaiting the coming rains so that they could be baptized. One man, Ole Mereru, especially showed change in his life. In the past, he had had the reputation of being a fighter, always ready with harsh arguments or worse. Though he had heard of the Gospel of peace, he had not yet let it take root and begin to freely work in him.

During our furlough he had made a solid break with his past way of life. Before an important cultural ceremony, the men from Ole Mereru's village, including Ole Mereru himself, had decided it best not to take part in the ceremony as they felt that some of the elements of it were in contradiction to their new faith. This decision provoked some other Maasai to anger. They told the men of Ole Mereru's village that they and their wives had to participate or pay the consequence of being beaten and ostracized.

Ole Mereru spoke up explaining why his village felt it would be wrong for them to join in certain events of the ceremony. The visitors pressed harder, saying that if they did not attend, the village would be fined some of its cattle. Ole Mereru held his ground, but did not shout or speak harshly as he had been accustomed to do in the past. He said, "You cannot fine us any animals, for we have done nothing wrong. We will give them to you, and we will come to the ceremony, but we will not join in the rites that we feel are contrary to our beliefs."

The visiting delegation was amazed at this change in Ole Mereru's usual behavior. They had expected a fight as a result of their charges and insults. But Ole Mereru had neither fought nor backed down from his position.

The families from Enkipang'asi that had moved out from the area were also growing in their faith. They reported that many other people in their new area were interested in receiving Christian teaching and that they themselves had many opportunities for evangelism.

When we had left the Loita Hills area in May of 1983, we had not seen many results from our three and a half years of ministry there. Now after our furlough we could see concrete evidence in the lives of many believers that their faith had grown and that they were reaching out beyond their own villages to those who have not yet heard. We feel blessed that the work continues.

Now our mission has asked us to go to Tanzania and begin a new work with a Maasai–speaking tribe there. Since we are going to a new country, a new area, and a new group of people, we will again adopt the role of learner. Such a role, we feel, is a proper role for a missionary or church worker today. Our Lord Himself said, "Unless you become as one of these ..."

◊

From the way Bruce and Cynthia took to the streets during the Language/Culture Learning & Mission course we were leading in Delhi, we were confident that they would do well using this approach to language learning and ministry. They are Belgians and had studied English earlier in a more traditional context.

Bruce and Cynthia have experienced some of the struggles that various non–school learners have experienced. It is not the food, the people or the climate that make it most difficult, but colleagues who are apparently uncomfortable when others live in local ways and experience deep relationships. As Bruce and Cynthia write, "During our first months we talked a lot about LAMP and our enthusiasm for our learning approach, but now we only talk about it when people ask us."

Their involvement in the life and community of the Nepali people, has developed deep friendships that have been mutually supportive. They were able to comfort their Nepali family on the death of the father, and the Nepalis ministered to the Hunters in their own hard times. These friendships have also given opportunities for sharing their life and faith.

The First Stumbling Steps

by Bruce and Cynthia Hunter

***LAMP* and** community-based language learning had not the least attraction for us the first time we heard about it. English study had been a headache for both of us even within the protection of a classroom. Now our mission was presenting us with a decision — on our arrival in Nepal we could follow the regular orientation and language study program or, if we were willing, we could be part of the first group of people in the mission to try an alternative method of learning language through relationships. All we remembered from our first introduction to the method was that we were to live with a Nepali family, limit our personal luggage to 20 kilos per person and use public transport only.

No thank you. Why should we? These kinds of Spartan conditions would obviously make life, and therefore language learning, unnecessarily complicated. The stresses of language learning and moving to a new country were great enough, why add to them by diving into the culture naked and defenseless?

For some reason — we still don't know why — we decided to go ahead with community–based language learning. In view of our prejudices and reluctance it was a totally illogical decision. We can only explain our step by believing we were overruled by God. Looking back, we feel that community–based language learning is one of the biggest blessings God has brought to our lives. By now, three years later, we have become burning "Lampers," and in some ways we would even consider our experience of learning through relationships to be almost as much a turning point as our conversion.

On the way to Nepal, we stopped in Delhi for a two–week training course under Tom and Betty Sue Brewster, who dealt with some of the prejudices harbored by our West European minds. After some encouragement, we were pushed out the door into the dusty streets of Delhi where we made an important discovery: language learning through relationships was *not* horrible. In fact, it worked delightfully well. By the end of the two–week course, we couldn't wait to get to Nepal and plunge in!

LEARNING IN KATHMANDU

And so it came to pass that on the 6th of February 1982 a small group of nine excited community–based language learners arrived from Delhi to take up the challenge of penetrating and becoming part of Kathmandu. We established a temporary base in a small hotel, and embarked on an exploration of the city. We walked its lanes and roads bubbling with activity, and the crowds immersed us in a wild variety of shouts, smells and sights. Our training in Delhi had equipped us in a practical way to survive and also to relate with and appreciate the local community.

After getting a rich taste of Kathmandu city life, the next steps on our agenda were to find a language helper who would help us learn a short text each day, and to build up a route of Nepali friends whom we could visit every day to practice with. On our second day in Nepal, Bruce found a superb helper who faithfully led him through Nepali for ten months until he had to move to another city. Cynthia found a helper a couple of weeks later. Gradually our route became established. We started from the teashop across from the cinema hall, included the chemist on the corner and the receptionists of the hotel, and often the tailor on the other side of the road. Soon we had about 20 to 30 different places we went to practice our texts.

After eight days in the hotel, our circle of friends had expanded and we were able to find one of the language learner's great blessings: a family willing to let us move in. It was a single–family household: husband, wife and two small children, and, as is normal in Nepal, lots of family members and friends were always drifting in and out.

We settled down in one room containing a cupboard of three drawers, a double mattress on the floor, one stool and our limited luggage. For the next two months that became our own little domain where we could withdraw from family life when necessary.

We also had the privilege of mingling in the family rooms any hour of the day. Among our precious memories are occasions like sitting in the little kitchen with the housewife seated on a very low bench cooking the traditional rice dish at 7 o'clock at night while listening to the babble of the two children. Or Cynthia doing the washing helped by the smallest of the two children. Or enjoying the songs and guitar-playing of the husband and his two younger brothers.

Those first two months we walked our route regularly and focussed mainly on pronunciation and fluency. We usually went on the route together, partly to be known as a married couple, and partly for mutual support. We each learned different texts to avoid boring people.

One day we were going home by a narrow lane that we had never tried before. After a few minutes we had a little tail of 4 or 5 children who were reciting one of our texts, one Bruce had been using several weeks before!

As time went on, and the Nepali language became less unintelligible, it became increasingly difficult for us to finish our route in time for the evening meal. The people

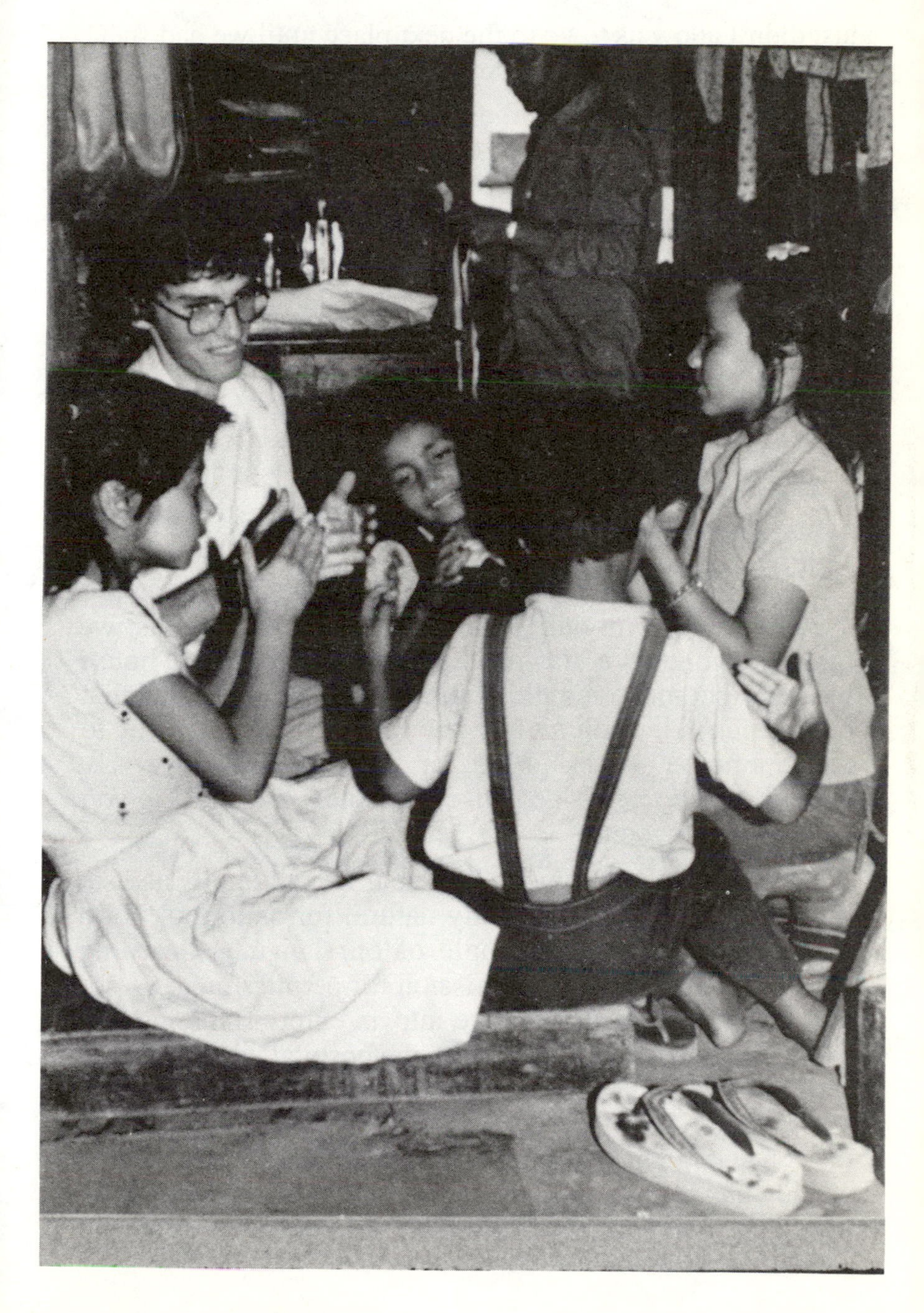

just didn't allow us to go to the next place until we had spent time with them, drunk this cup of tea, or tried that dish.

Clearly, it was not only the language we had to learn. We also needed to learn ... well, everything! How to eat, find a flat, buy things, react to sorrow and conflicts, and use a bus. How Nepali people think, what their concepts are about time, the supernatural, work, friendship, priorities of values. It was literally a whole new world with which we were totally unfamiliar.

We have found it essential to be known as learners by the local people, and not as Bruce, the dentist or Cynthia, the social worker. Being known as learners doesn't come with much glory or honor, but it is a role we prize.

FINDING A HOME

After living with our Nepali family for two months, we moved to our own flat on the ground floor of a house located right in the middle of our route. We were glad that our friends in the community had told us the Nepali way to locate a house — not by looking for a notice "to let," but rather by going from one house to the next asking, "Do you have an empty room?"

So when the time came to leave our Nepali family and set up our own house, it was only natural for us to look for a house right among the people of our language learning route. When we asked our mission for permission to do so, it was suggested that we move into an empty flat rented by the mission. The flat was close to the hospital where I would start working, but about five kilometers from our route. We felt that if we were to take that flat, we would lose all the contacts we had built up over the past months. That area already has many missionaries living in it, so there must be a witness there already, but we are the only ones here. So the mission agreed that we could move into a house along our route.

Of all the places we had seen, there were only two we considered. One was a flat in a house situated right in the middle of our route, on an important cross–road. The other was 10 minutes away and more isolated. We are certain that if we hadn't been learning language in the community, we would have opted for the second house — its privacy and quiet would have tipped the balance. But we chose, instead, the house on our route. Our flat was below road level with big windows so that people could look in and we could look out — an ideal place to learn. And our neighbors were people we knew already and with whom we could continue to build up relationships.

After two years in that house we moved a bit up our route. We felt we were ready for this next step. The place we live in now is an old–style Nepali house. We carry our water from the pump in front of the house and share the toilet with the other two families in the house — that's the way it's done.

Our Nepali friends began to find their way to our house. Visitors poured through in greater and greater numbers until it became next to impossible to get out on our route! Not wanting to lose our contacts on our language learning route, we followed a reduced schedule of our walking tours. Friends are always extending to us their generous hospitality and we love to reciprocate. Two families on our route even consider us as son and daughter-in-law.

COOKING, NEPALI STYLE

On setting up our first home, we found ourselves in quite a dilemma when we were generously provided with furniture. It was an issue we had not thought through, so we found ourselves with tables and chairs in our small, traditional kitchen, with the cooking space for our little kerosene stove on the floor.

When people started coming to our place, I (Cynthia) grew very unhappy about the whole set–up. As Nepalis don't enjoy sitting on chairs, and there was no floor-sitting space in our kitchen, I would leave them — even our closest friends — in our sitting room, while I would bustle around in the kitchen, fixing them tea. Opportunities and time for contact slipped through my fingers, especially when I was alone with visitors. Highly unsatisfactory. What could we do about it? Get rid of the table? This question caused an inner conflict. I was afraid that moving out our table would mean the loss of a very important atmosphere in our home — in Belgium, the best part of the day for sharing with family and friends is meal time and afterward, when people stay at the table chatting on and on.

We made it a matter of prayer and made a decision: out went the table. The enthusiasm of our Nepali friends was enormous. By getting rid of the table, we not only had made room for our friends to sit at ease on a *sukul* (large straw mat) in our kitchen, but also for the Nepali way of sitting and eating together. In Nepal, preparing the meal together in the cozy kitchen with close friends is the highlight of the visit! Then, right there in the kitchen, friends share the meal with each other, sitting around the dinner mat and learning about each other's lives.

When we had lived with our Nepali family, we had been dumbfounded when we noticed the lady cooking on a little stove placed on the floor. To her that was a normal and natural way to cook. To us, coming from the West, the idea of cooking on the floor had never even entered our heads! Living in close contact with that family gradually caused us to accept cooking on the floor as practical. What at first seemed impossible, became a possibility. We had become aware that a choice could be made — we could cook sitting on the floor the Nepali way, or we could cook standing, in the Belgian way. If we hadn't chosen to learn through relationships, we would have lived for those first months in a mission guesthouse where the Nepali helpers cook standing, and I certainly would have ended up cooking western–style food in a western way.

I think it is very important to decide from time to time what one is aiming for, what one's priorities are. Other women in the mission encouraged me to buy an oven, but I decided against it for I felt it would lead to baking Belgian pastry, spending too much time in my kitchen and not really trying to learn from Nepali friends how to make the tasty things they make — without an oven!

When we moved to our flat I decided to prepare at least one *'daal–bhaat'* (traditional Nepali rice meal) a day. But it didn't taste the way it should! Grinding spices and finding out the right amount or combination per dish proved very difficult. Cooking on the kerosene stove was also an adjustment for me. I was in tears more than once! I then made it a habit of asking advice from the woman in the vegetable shop whenever I did my shopping there: "How do you go about cooking these vegetables? What spices do you add? How much do you add of each?" She knows me as a person who asks "how, why, and when" all the time; she knows me as a learner. I've never stopped asking questions — and I found out why my *'daal'* (lentil soup) did not taste the way it should: first I should winnow the daal!

After doing the shopping I would sit down on the little stool in the kitchen to cook. Romila, a 9–year old friend, would often walk in and watch me. Soon she would wriggle, until she too was sitting on the little stool! I would watch her preparing our meal and, in doing so, learn a lot from her. She would feel proud, for she could do something that this grown woman couldn't. Thanks to her help in the beginning, as well as advice from shopkeepers and recipes from friends, we now eat delicious meals!

Some people say, "It's not all that important *how* we dress, or eat, or live, as long as we show them we love them. It's our attitude that's important!" We don't want to deny the last part of their statement, but can only express what a difference adjusting our lifestyle has made in our relationship with people here, and also within ourselves.

LOW POINTS

Our time here has not, however, been one long breathtaking Himalayan peak experience. The truth is, mountainous Nepal reminds us more of the ups and downs of our time here.

For one thing, the Nepali's pains have become our pains and their sorrows our sorrows. There were some relational problems in the family we stayed with. We thought it wise to share this experience with our mission colleagues. Their reaction was to feel sorry for us, because in their opinion we were enduring some unnecessary strains. It might have been wiser not to have mentioned it because later groups of language learners were not allowed to locate their own family. Instead, the mission picked out a family for the new missionaries. We ourselves considered it a privilege to have selected our own family to live with. Sure they have problems, but we came to Nepal to live among Nepalis and seek to meet their need.

Surprisingly, community–based language learning can have its times of real loneliness. To fulfill our call, we had chosen to live on our route and to spend as much time as possible with Nepalis. We had set our priorities and had to make some hard decisions about how we would spend our time. By making the choice to live on our route, we developed a lifestyle where we sought intensive contact with Nepalis, but this meant geographical isolation from missionary colleagues and little contact with them. At first, due to our limited language ability it was difficult to relate with Nepali friends on a deeper level, and due to our own choice we had little contact with mission colleagues on any level. So there were periods when we felt lonely because we had no one to deeply share and interact with.

After about four months in Nepal we reached our lowest point. Then we really had to face our loneliness. The immediate cause was another invitation to a social gathering of missionaries. We decided not to go. In our previous experiences with such meetings, although everybody speaks English, the conversations are on a rather superficial level and we invariably returned home feeling rather "empty." To relate to those in the expatriate community on a deeper and more personal level, we would have had to spend much more of our time with them, but we did not feel that should be our priority at the time.

I (Cynthia) found myself crying. Was contact with Nepali people worth this frustration? What would God have us do? At our wits' end, we brought our questions and pain before the Lord. Only minutes later, 11 year-old Sunsari looked at me and asked, "Why did you cry?" As best I could, I told her. Then she took two small plates from our cupboard and put a few sweets in each one, saying, "I came to bring you this." She had bought the sweets from her own scarce pocket–money.

Sunsari, a small Nepali girl, had turned one of the lowest points of our ministry into a joyful high! What a confirmation that was to our ministry. Whatever the cost, our call is to live with and learn from the group of Nepalis God has given us. Sunsari taught us that to live in relationships with people means to belong to each other and share in the events and sorrows of each other's lives.

When we heard about the death of *bua* (our Nepali father), we went straight to *ama* (our mother) and the rest of the family: an emergency situation in which simply being together was so important for all of us. Meeting the needs of one another in the way people do it here, is now our privilege.

EFFECTS ON OUR THEOLOGY AND MINISTRY

Both of us came to know the Lord personally as university students and joined a church that stressed the Bible as the Word of God. We accepted Jesus' birth, life, sacrificial death on the cross and His coming again soon, and the importance of a personal relationship with God. As part of the package, mission was defined as the verbal proclamation of the Gospel overseas. On many problems and questions that came up in our church, there was no discussion, just one solitary "biblical" answer.

Now, only a few years later, we see that several perspectives of our faith have been modified, as our new environment and a new learning approach have thrown a new light on our ideals.

A Buddhist here told us, "One of the weaknesses of the west is that it ignores the spiritual realm, but in Nepal the spiritual and material world are interwoven." Here in Nepal, there is an acute awareness of spiritual forces. Good and bad gods and spirits are present everywhere; they communicate with people, in dreams for instance, and through people like mediums and witch doctors. Diseases are believed to be caused by the influences of gods, spirits, curses, and witchcraft. So when they become ill, most Nepali people will consult a medium where the prophesying spirit or god informs the sufferer of the cause, course and duration of the disease, or to a local healer who possesses supernatural power. Often they do get well. Our theology hadn't prepared us to deal with that.

Although we have had a de facto belief in spiritual things, God is using the Nepali awareness of the spiritual realm to show us we have much to learn in this area.

Many Christians, including ourselves in the past, spend their time with and for each other — in prayer meetings, teaching, and worship. We were overly concerned with ourselves, and wouldn't have anything to do with the world — it was sinful and bad. Because we were not interested in politics and global issues we were unable to discuss these topics, and unable to make an impact on Belgian society.

Interestingly enough, we have found a parallel situation in the national church in Nepal. The national church seems to be an island to itself, in an area that is virtually 99 percent Hindu. In our local church here, the members are certainly not representative of the local population. Many are expatriate Asians and Westerners. The leader of the church is not Nepali, and the pattern of the service is western. Everything that faintly smells of Hinduism is out.

For example, Christmas is celebrated by Christians here on December 25th. But at the end of November the Hindu people celebrate *Tihaar,* the Festival of Light. Could the church give this festival a Christian meaning? Is not Christmas our Festival of the Light that came to the world?

Traditionally in Nepal, the sari worn by a bride is red, that being the color which symbolizes the presence of a god or goddess. A Christian bride will wear a white gown on her wedding day. Yet white, here in Nepal, is the color for widows and others who have lost a close relative by death. Would it be appropriate for Christian Nepali brides to wear red?

Christian women do not wear *sindur,* the red powder applied in the parting of the hair, which means a woman is married and also that the wife recognizes her husband as her god.[1] We sometimes wonder what would happen to one of our married friends if she wished to become a member of the church. If she were to join the local church here, she would be expected to take off the sindur, never to wear it again. Our guess is that her dearest would give her a good beating when she came home. What else could one expect if she no longer wanted to wear his "wedding ring?"

We now find ourselves struggling with the question: How has God been preparing these people for Himself? Has God been present in some ways in Hinduism? Where do values such as love and justice in Hindu culture come from — can these be bridges to faith in Christ? How can customs such as the purification rituals that speak of God's love and mercy be used to bring Nepalis to an understanding of salvation?

The way Christians give shape to their Christian faith should be determined within each local culture. The forms are not universal. Practices from one culture should not be imposed on another.

It became quite clear very soon after we arrived in Nepal that our practiced and perfected Belgian methods of verbal gospel proclamation were useless in Nepal. There is no question — first one learns, and then one can communicate. This communicating may then turn out to be very different from what we had expected.

On our language route we got to know many people, more than we ever imagined we would. They are, we believe, precious gifts from God. Our call is to live with them, learn from them and share with them. And we see God at work. ◊

---

[1]*Sindur* is applied the first time during the wedding ceremony. The husband makes a red line in the partition of his young bride's hair. From then onwards she is officially his wife. Then, daily she will draw this red line in her hair.

What we give up for Christ we gain.
What we keep back for ourselves is our real loss.
— *Hudson Taylor*, on Philippians 3

A Post Script from the Editors

Your editors hope this book has been an encouragement to you. Maybe now you can say with optimism, "I think I could learn a language and enjoy ministering *this* way."

We usually feel it is best for most North Americans to be pre-trained before they attempt community language learning. This enables them to demonstrate that they are ready to take the initiative and be responsible for their own learning relationships, strategies and skills. We suspect, however, that given the right training, attitude and opportunity, all of us probably have the ability to become bilingual and bicultural.

Each summer we teach an intensive two-week course in Language/Culture Learning and Mission at the Fuller School of World Mission in Pasadena, CA (and elsewhere by invitation). The course content is designed to give skills for language and culture learning along with missiological perspective for effective cross-cultural ministry. Write to the adddress below if you would like more information.

In addition to ***Community Is My Language Classroom!*** we have prepared the following materials for missionary language learners: ***Language Acquisition Made Practical*** (***LAMP***) — a how-to book for language learning; ***Language Exploration & Acquisition Resource Notebook!*** (***LEARN!***); ***Bonding and the Missionary Task*** (includes "Language Learning *Is* Communication — *Is* Ministry"); and ***Language Learning & Mission*** — a 10-hour introductory video series. These and other materials are available from Lingua House Ministries, Box 91, Fuller Station, Pasadena, CA 91182.

May the Lord bless you as serve Him.

Tom and Betty Sue Brewster

God bless you!